VIENNESE CUISINE

VIENNESE CUISINE

THE NEW APPROACH

Peter Grunauer
Andreas Kisler

WITH
Donald Flanell Friedman

PHOTOGRAPHS BY
Ernest Richter

Doubleday

NEW YORK

1987

Library of Congress Cataloging-in-Publication Data
Grunauer, Peter, 1950–
   Viennese cuisine.
   Includes index.
   1. Cookery, Austrian. 2. Cookery—Austria—Vienna.
I. Kisler, Andreas. II. Friedman, Donald Flanell.
III. Title.
TX721.G684 1987   641.59436'13   87-9253
ISBN 0-385-27999-X

Contents

Preface

A perfect balance of delicacy and sensuousness of flavor characterizes modern Viennese cooking. The refinement of this cuisine is the culmination of the long evolution of Viennese cooking, always multinational in character. As the capital of the Hapsburg empire, Vienna was the convergence point of an immense realm that extended from the Adriatic to the borders of Russia. Hapsburgs governed not only the contemporary Eastern European nations of Hungary, Czechoslovakia, and parts of Yugoslavia and Romania, but also at various epochs during their six-hundred-year reign, much of northern Italy, Sicily, Sardinia, Spain, Flanders, Burgundy, Mexico, and Peru, among other areas. No fewer than sixteen languages were spoken in the empire before the outbreak of the First World War. Viennese cuisine naturally expressed and was enriched by the most varied influences.

Peter Grunauer's own background reflects this spirit of internationalism. He grew up in an environment in which food was a passionate interest. As soon as he was old enough to reach the tables, he waited on customers at his parents' popular restaurant in Vienna's Seventh District, which specializes in traditional Austrian cooking. Mr. Grunauer, a skilled chef as well as a restaurateur, was trained on two continents, studying at the Hotel School in Vienna and at Cornell University in the United States. He has worked for many years with creative chef Andreas Kisler, trained at the restaurant of the Palais Schwarzenberg, citadel of elegant dining in Vienna, as well as at La Marée, one of the finest seafood restaurants in Paris. This cross-fertilization of Austrian and French culinary ideas is also rooted in tradition. During the 1815 Congress of Vienna, Talleyrand brought a potent diplomatic weapon to Austria, the chef Marie-Antoine Carême, who became the master of the *grand cuisine* of Europe. Like the renowned epicure Brillat-Savarin, Andy Kisler believes that "the discovery of a new dish does more for the happiness of the human race than the discovery of a star." Emphasizing the freshest herbs and choicest ingredients, many of the recipes in this book are Mr. Kisler's transformations and interpretations of the traditional. In 1985 he was the youngest of the ten chefs chosen to appear on PBS television's "The Master Chefs of New York."

Peter Grunauer hopes to bring about a renaissance of Austrian cooking and to make a statement about fine dining. He strongly denies the identification of Austrian cooking with overly assertive peasant fare. He believes that contemporary Austrian cuisine must be true to its heritage by continuing to evolve, developing into the gourmet fare of today: food that is light, plentiful, and beautifully served, exciting to look at, enticing to the appetite. Peter Grunauer conceives of a meal as a feast for all the senses: beginning with the keynote of the appetizer, to awaken the palate, harmoniously developed through the main course, and culminating in one of the celestial desserts for which Vienna is justly famed. This new approach to cooking represents a culinary celebration of life's abundance, the profusion of its good things, and also of finesse.

Donald Flanell Friedman

Introduction

Gemütlichkeit could be said to be our Austrian attitude toward living. The word is difficult to translate literally, but implies a relaxed and knowledgeable enjoyment of all the pleasures of life. Cooking, basic and vital for suvival, is an art form. Your special dinner should be an event that lingers in memory, a source of delight to you and your guests.

It was several years ago that I first decided to write a book which, I hoped, would change your ideas about Viennese cooking. It is evident that we live in a health-conscious age. Chef Andreas Kisler and I believe that Austrian food need not be only the hearty fare enjoyable on a winter's day. Such dishes, of course, have an important place on the menu, and you will find recipes in our book for the best of the traditional favorites. There are times, however, when you will decide to serve food that is light without sacrificing flavor. We are convinced that our light versions of Viennese classics gain in flavor from the very delicacy of the sauces, made by reduction, without any flour or thickener, and the refinement with which we combine choice ingredients.

You will find that we have included many interesting and creative recipes for fish, one of the healthiest protein sources. Before World War I, Austria had territory on the Adriatic and was supplied with a profusion of seafood. True to the spirit of the past, when fish markets flourished in Vienna, I have a great variety and quantity of fresh seafood flown to my restaurant daily from around the world.

Because of its lightness and subtlety, seafood makes an ideal first course. You may want to establish a sense of progression in your meal by complementing a seafood appetizer with a main course such as our rosy Lamb Fillets with Mint Sauce enhanced by an array of bright vegetables. Bear in mind while following our recipes that all tastes should maintain their integrity while combining to form a remarkable whole. The composite flavor of the dish must be that of the products used in making it. For this reason you should use only the best and freshest products available. Remember to let the time of year and availability of fine ingredients help you decide which recipes to choose. Why defeat your effort to prepare something special by using an inferior cut of meat or canned or frozen produce?

A word about dessert, which is an integral part of dinner in Austria: Vienna is famous the world over for its coffeehouses and pastry shops where you can sit for hours, sipping a wide variety of coffees and sampling sweets. Here we share our versions of the beloved pastries, in recipes in which the quantity of flour has often been reduced, enabling even the serious weight watcher to indulge in the inimitable pleasure of a Viennese dessert. As an unusual ending to a special dinner, you might want to serve your guests our Kapuziner Palatschinken, crepes filled with warm chestnut puree and complemented by chocolate sauce, or our Topfenknödel, fluffy little farmer cheese dumplings in a gleaming fruit sauce. You might decide to arrange small portions of several desserts on a plate—a tiny square of dark chocolate Sachertorte, contrasting with a creamy little dollop of mousse and a cloud of frozen Praline Parfait, the whole set off with refreshing crescents of melon.

I hope you will enjoy the blend of the traditional Austrian and international cuisine that my chef, Andreas Kisler, and I have developed. We wish you great pleasure in preparing and serving our recipes. You won't need to know any special techniques or culinary secrets. You need only be willing to relax and enjoy the process of cooking. I believe that there is no greater pleasure in life than preparing a wonderful meal for your guests and enjoying it in their company.

                                                        Peter Grunauer

New York City
July 1985

CHAPTER 1

Appetizers

Beautiful colors and appealing presentation are essential for the first course, the moment of the meal that establishes a relaxed mood of conviviality, pleasurable surprise, and anticipation of the culinary adventure to follow.

In all of our appetizers, flavors maintain their integrity and natural distinction. These dishes represent our style, a mixture of the traditional Viennese, variations on classic themes, and our own innovations. Healthy seafood abounds. Our seafood salads and terrines can be made a day in advance of your dinner party, and many of our appetizers can be served as main courses.

VIENNESE CHANTERELLES

SERVES 6

A wide variety of European mushrooms are now available in specialty food shops in the United States. The dainty chanterelle, known for its egg-yolk-yellow color and slightly peppery taste, is particularly prized in Viennese cuisine. When vacationing in the Austrian countryside, one can awaken early after a summer rainstorm and hunt through cool, scented pine forests for this treat. The following is a traditional recipe that you will find makes a delicious appetizer or light main dish. Try it with a crusty black bread to soak up the rich mushroom cream. Our recommendation for an appropriate wine is Austrian Pinot Blanc by Klosterkeller Siegendorf or a good Mâcon Villages.

8 tablespoons butter
2 medium onions, finely diced
1 1/2 pounds chanterelles, rinsed, dried on paper towels, and torn by hand into quarters
1/2 cup heavy cream
1 tablespoon fresh thyme, or to taste
Salt and freshly ground white pepper to taste
6 eggs
1/2 bunch parsley (leaves only), rinsed, dried, and finely chopped

1. In a skillet, heat 6 tablespoons of the butter, add the onions, and sauté for 5 minutes over high heat. Add the chanterelles and sauté for 5 more minutes.

2. Add the heavy cream to the skillet, cover, and allow to simmer over low heat for about 5 minutes, until the chanterelles are tender.

3. Season with the thyme and salt and pepper to taste. Leave the skillet uncovered and keep warm over low heat.

4. Meanwhile, in a separate pan, fry the 6 eggs in the remaining 2 tablespoons butter, sunny side up. Drain on paper towels.

5. Arrange the chanterelles on warm plates. Sprinkle with the chopped parsley and top each portion with a fried egg.

WARM DUCK SALAD WITH GREEN BEANS

SERVES 6

This pairing of warm, savory duck and crisp, cold green beans is a year-round favorite.

1 (5–6-pound) duck
1¹/₂ pounds green beans, tips removed
¹/₃ cup olive oil
4 tablespoons sherry vinegar
4 mushroom caps, thinly sliced
4 shallots, peeled and thinly sliced
¹/₈ teaspoon fresh thyme
2 bay leaves
10 black peppercorns
Salt and freshly ground white pepper to taste

1. Preheat the oven to 375° F.
2. Roast the duck for 2 hours, until golden brown. Remove the duck legs and breast. Set aside to cool. Reserve the rest of the duck for another recipe.
3. While the duck is roasting, bring 2 quarts of salted water to a boil in a large pot and add the beans. Boil for 4 to 5 minutes until cooked, but still crisp. Refresh in ice water to retain their bright color, then drain.
4. In a glass bowl, combine the olive oil, 2 tablespoons of the vinegar, the mushrooms, shallots, thyme, bay leaves, and peppercorns. Season with salt and pepper to taste, toss well, and set aside to marinate at room temperature for at least 1 hour.
5. Pour the remaining 2 tablespoons vinegar into a separate glass bowl. Season with salt and pepper to taste. Add the green beans, toss well to coat, and set aside to marinate at room temperature for at least 1 hour.
6. Bone the duck legs, and carve them into thin slices. Julienne the duck breast.
7. To serve, drain the vegetables, and combine the 2 marinades. Arrange equal portions of vegetables on 6 individual plates. Cover with slices of duck meat and drizzle marinade over all.

BREAST OF CHICKEN POACHED WITH HERBS

SERVES 6

Chicken breasts are poached in a broth perfumed with fresh tarragon, basil, and rosemary. Fragrant peppermint adds a sparkling note. Served with refreshing, colorful crescents of melon and topped with a silken honey and lemon dressing, this makes an enticing appetizer or a light main course. You need serve nothing more than good French bread and a well-chilled, fruity white wine. We recommend Sauvignon Blanc by Klosterkeller Siegendorf, or Napa Valley Chardonnay by Burgess Cellars.

1 egg yolk
1 teaspoon honey
2 tablespoons white vinegar
Juice of 1 lemon
Salt and pepper to taste
1/4 cup grape-seed oil or olive oil
2 whole chicken breasts, with bones removed and reserved
    for making broth*
2 tablespoons each fresh, coarsely chopped tarragon,
    peppermint, basil, and rosemary, mixed together (if
    fresh herbs are absolutely not available, use 1
    tablespoon each dried herbs)
6 lettuce leaves (such as Bibb, romaine, or escarole)
1 medium cantaloupe, cut lengthwise into halves, with
    seeds removed, cut from the peel, and cut lengthwide
    into 1/2-inch slices

1. Mix the egg yolk, honey, vinegar, and lemon juice in a bowl. When blended, season with salt and pepper to taste. Add the oil slowly, drop by drop, whisking gently until the dressing is thick and smooth. Set aside.

2. Place the bones from the chicken breasts in a pot and cover with 4 cups of water. Add all of the herbs. Bring to a boil, immedi-

* If making the chicken broth is too time-consuming, you may substitute bouillon cubes dissolved in water or canned chicken broth. You'll need about 2 cups.

ately lower the heat, and simmer over low heat, uncovered, until the liquid is reduced to 2 cups.

3. Strain the broth through cheesecloth and then skim the grease from the top of the strained broth. Remove 2 tablespoons of the broth, allow to cool, and then stir into the prepared dressing.

4. Bring the remaining broth to a boil in a large skillet. If you are using prepared broth, add the herbs now to poach with the chicken. Add the chicken breasts, cover, and simmer over low heat for 6 to 8 minutes.

5. Remove the poached chicken from the broth and allow to cool. Cut the chicken into 1-inch cubes.

6. Place a lettuce leaf on each chilled plate; cover with chicken cubes and garnish attractively with the melon slices. Pour the dressing over the tips of the melon slices and the chicken cubes and lettuce.

SWEETBREADS AND FOIE GRAS
ON SEASONAL SALAD

SERVES 6

This uncomplicated dish is simple to prepare and a fine way to begin a winter meal. Delicate, golden sweetbreads, alternated with slices of rich, savory foie gras, are given an unusual tangy accent with a sherry vinegar dressing.

1 pound sweetbreads, repeatedly rinsed in running water, with lining and sinews removed, and then refreshed in ice water
Flour for coating
1 pound fresh or vacuum-packed foie gras (do not use canned)
1 whole egg
1/4 cup walnut oil, plus 1/3 cup for sautéing
1 egg yolk
4 tablespoons sherry vinegar
Salt and freshly ground white pepper to taste
Fresh seasonal lettuce leaves

1. Slice the cleaned sweetbreads into 12 pieces. Dip both sides of the sweetbread pieces in the flour. Pat the slices to prevent the flour from clumping. Slice the foie gras also into 12 pieces, and flour.

2. Whisk the whole egg in a bowl and dip each floured slice of sweetbread in the egg. Dip the foie gras in flour only.

3. Heat 1/3 cup of the walnut oil in a skillet and sauté the slices over medium heat until golden. You will probably need to do this in batches. Keep the cooked slices warm on a covered plate.

4. Meantime, mix the egg yolk and sherry vinegar in a bowl. Add the remaining walnut oil, drop by drop, whisking continuously, until blended and creamy. Season with salt and white pepper to taste.

5. Arrange lettuce leaves in the center of each plate. Drizzle the dressing onto the lettuce. Place 2 warm slices each of sweetbread and foie gras on the plate surrounding the salad, like the points of a compass.

SCALLOPS IN A VERMOUTH AND SAFFRON SAUCE

SERVES 6

Fresh pink grapefruit adds zest and a hint of exoticism to these classic scallops, gilded with saffron.

Oil for sautéing, preferably corn or safflower
1 pound bay scallops (about—you will need 30 scallops)
2 shallots, peeled and finely diced
1/4 cup dry vermouth
1 cup heavy cream
Pinch of saffron
Juice of 1 lemon
Salt and freshly ground white pepper to taste
2 pink grapefruits, peeled and sectioned

1. In a skillet, heat approximately 2 tablespoons of the oil to sizzling and sauté the scallops until tender and juicy to the fork, not more than 2 minutes. Remove the scallops and place in a covered dish to keep warm.

2. Pour 1 tablespoon fresh oil into the skillet and sauté the shallots until transparent.

3. Add the vermouth and reduce over medium-high heat until 2 tablespoons are left.

4. Add the cream and saffron. Reduce by half over low heat, to a creamy sauce consistency. Season with the lemon juice and with salt and pepper to taste.

5. Strain the sauce through a fine sieve and discard the shallots.

6. Pour the sauce onto 6 warm plates. Arrange 5 scallops in a cross pattern on each plate. Place 1 grapefruit section between each 2 arms of the cross.

SALMON AND SCALLOP SALAD

SERVES 6

This summery cool seafood salad, which is also a fine main dish, can be made a day in advance of your dinner party and refrigerated.

You will find an elegant clarity in the very preparation of this dish. The seafood is first poached in wine, vermouth, and seasonings. String beans are then briefly cooked in the fish stock that results from the poaching. Finally a tarragon mayonnaise, itself thinned with some stock, is added to the dish. Everything blends in a memorable way.

1/2 cup dry white wine
1/2 cup dry vermouth
2 bay leaves
6 peppercorns
1/2 pound fresh salmon, cut into 1/2-inch cubes
6 sea scallops
1 pound small string beans, rinsed, with both tips snapped off
6 shallots, peeled and finely sliced
2 scallions (both white and green parts), cut into 1/2-inch pieces
2 egg yolks
1 teaspoon tarragon vinegar
1/2 cup good olive oil
Salt and freshly ground white pepper to taste

1. Bring the wine, vermouth, l cup of water, the bay leaves, and peppercorns to a boil in a saucepan. Add the salmon cubes and scallops, then immediately lower the heat and simmer 3 to 4 minutes. (Never allow fish to boil, for overcooking will ruin its flavor.)

2. Remove the seafood from the stock and set aside to cool. Leave the stock on very low heat.

3. Cook the string beans 6 to 8 minutes in the simmering fish stock. The beans should remain quite crisp.

4. Remove the beans and set the stock aside to cool. Refresh the beans in a bowl of ice water and drain.

5. When the stock is cool, add the green beans, shallots, and scallions and refrigerate.

6. Mix the egg yolks and vinegar in a bowl. Drop by drop, add the olive oil, whisking the entire time, until the dressing thickens to the consistency of mayonnaise.

7. Thin the dressing by stirring in 3 tablespoons of the refrigerated fish stock. Season with salt and pepper to taste.

8. To serve, remove the green bean mixture from the stock. Place the mixture in a bowl with the poached salmon, add the salad dressing, and mix gently. Distribute among 6 plates and garnish each with a scallop.

BAY SCALLOPS AND CRAYFISH SALAD, SERVED WITH CANTALOUPE AND PINK GRAPEFRUIT SECTIONS

SERVES 6

An intriguing combination of fruit and seafood, this is also a fabulous main dish, serving four. The scallops and crayfish are marinated in a dressing redolent with tarragon, apples, and walnuts. Louisiana crayfish, those spiky crustaceans, are now to be found not only in specialty food stores but in most fish markets. If they are not available, shrimp are a perfect substitute.

1 pound bay scallops
Dry white wine for poaching
12 live crayfish (or 12 large shrimp)
3 egg yolks
1 tablespoon tarragon vinegar
2 tablespoons walnut oil
2 cups sour cream
2 peeled and cored Granny Smith apples, cut into 1-inch
    cubes
2 tablespoons walnuts, chopped
2 tablespoons finely chopped fresh tarragon (1 tablespoon
    dried tarragon may be used if necessary)
6 medium tomatoes, peeled, with seeds removed, cut into
    1-inch cubes
Salt and freshly ground white pepper to taste
Juice of 1 lemon (about)
2 pink grapefruits
1 small cantaloupe

1. Place the bay scallops in a skillet and add enough wine to cover. Heat over a moderate flame until the scallops are lightly poached, about 7 to 8 minutes. They should remain tender and juicy to the fork. Remove the scallops and set aside, leaving the stock in the pan.

2. Boil the live crayfish in the scallop stock for 1 minute. Re-

move the crayfish and cool them in ice water. Carefully break the tails in half and remove the meat. Place the crayfish meat in the bowl with the scallops and set aside.

3. In a bowl, mix together the egg yolks and tarragon vinegar. Add the walnut oil, drop by drop, whisking the while, until it reaches a mayonnaise consistency. Stir in the sour cream. If the dressing is too thick, add some of the fish stock, a little at a time.

4. Add the apples, walnuts, tarragon, and tomatoes. Stir. Mix the crayfish and scallops into the dressing. Add salt, pepper, and lemon juice to taste. Refrigerate.

5. Peel the grapefruits and section them. Peel the cantaloupe, cut in half, remove the seeds, and thinly slice it. Arrange the fruit attractively on one side of 6 chilled plates. Nestle the seafood salad alongside.

RAGOUT OF CRAYFISH TAILS, CHANTERELLES, AND OYSTERS

SERVES 6

Ragouts (from the French *ragoûter,* "to revive the taste") were traditionally served between courses to stimulate the appetite.
    A dry Chardonnay may be served.

**36 live crayfish, boiled in salted water for 2 minutes, then
        refreshed in ice water**
Dry white wine for boiling the oysters
12 Belon oysters, rinsed
1 cup heavy cream
1/3 cup oil for sautéing
4 shallots, peeled and finely sliced
**11/4 cups chanterelles, rinsed, patted dry with paper towels,
        and torn in half**
2 tablespoons cognac
1/2 teaspoon fresh thyme
1 clove garlic, peeled
Juice of 1 lemon
Salt and freshly ground white pepper to taste

1. Remove the meat from the boiled crayfish tails and set aside.
Reserve 6 crayfish heads with claws for garnishing.

2. In a saucepan, bring white wine sufficient to cover the oysters to a boil. Add the oysters and continue boiling until they open.
Remove the oyster meat from the shells and set aside.

3. Continue boiling the wine until reduced by half. Add the
heavy cream and continue boiling until reduced by half, then simmer, uncovered, over low heat.

4. Heat the oil in a saucepan and sauté the shallots and chanterelles over medium heat for 7 to 8 minutes. Add the cognac and
reduce almost all of the liquid. Stir in the thyme and the garlic clove.
Add the lemon juice and remove the garlic. Add the reduced cream
and bring to a boil for a moment. Add the crayfish and oysters to the
sauce and stir. Season with salt and pepper to taste.

5. Arrange the shellfish ragout attractively in the center of 6

large, warm plates. Garnish each portion with a reserved crayfish head.

VIENNESE SNAIL SALAD

SERVES 6

When we think of snails, the standard garlic and butter preparation comes first to mind. Although known as a French food, snails have long been appreciated in Austrian cuisine. We find this snail salad a welcome and satisfying change.

48 snails, without their shells, rinsed and drained
3 tablespoons wine vinegar
6 tablespoons salad oil, preferably corn or safflower
Salt and freshly ground black pepper to taste
6 eggs, hard-boiled, peeled and chopped*
1 tablespoon freshly grated horseradish†
1 white onion, peeled and finely diced
6 fresh green lettuce leaves, cut into a chiffonade (thin,
    straight strips, equal in size)

1. Reserve 6 whole snails for garnishing, and then cut the other snails into thin slices.

2. Prepare a marinade by mixing the wine vinegar, salad oil, and salt and pepper to taste.

3. Place the whole and sliced snails in the marinade for 10 minutes.

4. Remove the 6 whole snails from the marinade and set aside.

5. Carefully add the chopped egg, horseradish, and onion to the snail marinade. Gently fold all of the ingredients together.

6. Arrange the lettuce attractively on 6 chilled plates. Place the prepared snail salad on the lettuce and pour some marinade over each serving. Garnish each portion with 1 whole snail.

* Boil the eggs for 6 minutes and then place immediately in cold water in order to remove the shells easily.

† Peel the skin from the horseradish root with a small paring knife, then rub the root against the fine side of a grater.

MUSSELS WITH PAPAYA IN A
POMMERY MUSTARD DRESSING

SERVES 6

This voluptuous combination of seafood, cooling papaya slices, and a velvety mustard dressing is also a fine main dish for a light luncheon or supper. We use New Zealand mussels. While once the kiwi fruit imported from New Zealand was a rarity, now it's widely available in markets. Similarly, the enormous, intense, and succulent New Zealand mussels will become increasingly available. If you cannot find the New Zealand variety, we recommend using cultivated mussels, which tend to be cleaner than ordinary mussels and closer in flavor to the giant New Zealand beauties.

A dry white wine may accompany this dish. Our recommendation is Grüner Veltliner by Bruendelmayer-Malat, or Napa Valley Chardonnay by Robert Mondavi.

18 large New Zealand mussels or 42 mussels
1/3 cup oil for sautéing
4 shallots, peeled and cut à la Julienne (into thin slices)
1 cup dry white wine
1 bay leaf
5 black peppercorns
3 ripe papayas

POMMERY MUSTARD DRESSING
2 egg yolks
1 tablespoon tarragon vinegar
1 cup olive oil
1/2 cup salad oil, preferably corn or safflower
4–5 tablespoons Pommery mustard
1/2 cup sour cream
Salt and freshly ground white pepper to taste

1. Rinse the mussels under cold running water and debeard them.

2. Heat the oil in a kettle over high flame. Lower the flame, add the shallots, and sauté until they are transparent.

3. Add the mussels and sauté them quickly, stirring, until the shells open.

4. Add the wine, bay leaf, peppercorns, and enough water to cover the mussels completely. Bring to a boil, lower the flame, cover the pot, and allow to simmer for about 7 minutes.

5. Remove the mussels from the kettle and cool them in ice water. Pull the mussels from their shells and set aside.

6. Meanwhile, bring the liquid back to a boil and reduce to a quarter of the original amount, producing a thick stock. Strain off the bay leaf and peppercorns. Allow the stock to cool, and set aside.

7. Prepare the dressing: whisk the egg yolks and vinegar in a salad bowl. Add the olive oil drop by drop, whisking all the while. Then stir in the salad oil. Next fold in the mustard and sour cream. Finally dilute the dressing by stirring in 1/4 cup of the cool reserved mussel stock. Season with salt and pepper to taste.

8. Place the mussels in the dressing and marinate for 10 minutes.

9. Meanwhile, halve and peel the papayas and cut into thin slices. Arrange the papaya slices in attractive fan shapes on 6 chilled plates. Remove the mussels from the dressing and put 2 New Zealand or 7 regular mussels on each plate. Coat the mussels and tips of the papaya slices with the Pommery mustard dressing.

CALF'S HEAD IN ASPIC WITH A
RED ONION VINAIGRETTE

SERVES 16

In Austria, calf's head in aspic, known as "Sulz," is traditional fare often served in *Heuriger,* the wine gardens where good cheer is celebrated in a pastoral surrounding. Friends will drive to the wine-growing suburbs of Vienna, Grinzing or Nussdorf, to gather for walks and sit around wooden tables beneath the trees, relaxing and enjoying hearty fare and wine. Tangy and sour, this Sulz with a piquant red onion vinaigrette is a flavorful accompaniment for a bacchanalian bout of drinking. It is a striking addition to a cold buffet and makes great picnic food. Serve with plenty of cold, full-bodied blond beer or with refreshing spritzers made with chilled white wine and soda.

1/2 calf's head (ask your butcher to cut the head
    lengthwise)
1 white onion, larded with 2 bay leaves and 10 whole
    cloves
20 black peppercorns
1 medium carrot, peeled and cut into small cubes
1 medium yellow turnip, peeled and cut into small cubes
2 cornichons, diced
3 egg whites, at room temperature
2 sheets gelatin or 2 envelopes unflavored gelatin,
    dissolved in 1/2 cup cold water
2 tablespoons wine vinegar
Salt and freshly ground white pepper to taste
Lettuce leaves

RED ONION VINAIGRETTE
1 medium red onion, peeled and cut into very small cubes
1 teaspoon Dijon mustard
1/4 cup wine vinegar
3/4 cup olive oil
1 small bunch each of parsley, chives, and chervil, washed,
    dried, and finely chopped
Salt and freshly ground white pepper to taste

1. Clean the calf's head of any remaining hair. Blanch the head by placing it in boiling salted water for 2 minutes. Remove and rinse in cold water.

2. Place the blanched calf's head in a pot, cover with water, and bring to a boil.

3. Add the larded onion and peppercorns. Boil for 15 minutes. Add the carrot and turnip and continue boiling until the meat and vegetables are tender, about 35 minutes. The meat should come off the bone easily.

4. Remove the meat and vegetables from the pot. Discard the onion and peppercorns. Reserve the stock.

5. Pull the meat from the bone and then chop into 1/2-inch cubes. Mix the meat, carrot, and turnip cubes in a bowl. Add the cubed cornichons. Place this mixture in a 2-quart terrine and allow to cool.

6. Boil the reserved stock down until about 1 cup remains; the reduced stock should be thick. Remove from the heat.

7. Whip the egg whites until they are stiff and stir them into the warm, thickened stock. Slowly bring to a boil over medium heat.

8. Stir the dissolved gelatin into the boiling mixture and remove from the heat. Season with the wine vinegar and salt and white pepper to taste.

9. Generously cover the meat and vegetables in the terrine with the gelatin mixture. Cool to room temperature, then refrigerate at least 3 hours.

10. Prepare the vinaigrette: mix the onion, mustard, and vinegar in a bowl. Add the oil, drop by drop, whisking all the while. Stir in the parsley, chives, and chervil. Season with salt and pepper to taste.

11. Place 2 thin slices of the aspic on lettuce leaves on each plate. Drizzle with a tablespoon of the vinaigrette.

TAGLIOLINI AND TAGLIATELLE

Pasta and seafood combinations have become increasingly popular. Here are a few of the more interesting and elegant variations. All can double as appetizers or main-dish suppers. The perfect wine to serve with these pasta courses is Cabernet Merlot by R. Schlumberger.

BASIC RECIPE FOR TAGLIOLINI AND TAGLIATELLE

SERVES 12

Tagliatelle are ½ inch wide and 1 foot long. Tagliolini are of the same width as spaghetti and 15 inches long.

2 cups plus 2 tablespoons fine-ground semolina flour
2 cups plus 2 tablespoons all-purpose flour
1 teaspoon salt
5 eggs
1 tablespoon olive oil

1. Sift together the flours and the salt. Place the flour mixture in a mound on a clean surface. Make a well in the center and put the eggs and oil in the well. Work the liquid ingredients into the flour with your hands. Knead the dough until thoroughly blended. The dough should be firm.

2. Allow the dough to rest for 1 hour and then put through a pasta machine.

TAGLIATELLE WITH SMOKED SALMON
AND GREEN PEAS

SERVES 6

1 pound tagliatelle, packaged or homemade
3/4 pound fresh green peas
2 tablespoons olive oil
6 ounces smoked salmon, cut into 1/2-inch cubes
2 tablespoons vodka
1/2 cup heavy cream
Salt and freshly ground white pepper to taste
Juice of 1/2 lemon (about)

1. Boil the pasta in plenty of salted water until done "al dente," tender but firm. Strain and refresh in ice water to halt the cooking. Set aside.

2. Meantime, shell the peas, then boil 1 minute in salted water, drain, and refresh in ice water.

3. Heat the olive oil in a large saucepan and sauté the salmon over medium heat for 3 to 4 minutes. Add the vodka and reduce for 2 to 3 minutes. Then add the cream and bring to a simmer.

4. Add the peas and season with salt, pepper, and lemon juice to taste.

5. While the sauce is still simmering, add the tagliatelle. Stir the pasta in the sauce a few times to coat it.

6. Serve immediately in warm soup plates.

TAGLIOLINI WITH LOBSTER, SHRIMP, AND CRAYFISH

SERVES 6

If fresh crayfish are not available, this dish is just as delicious with either lobster or shrimp alone.

1 (1½-pound) live lobster
4 live crayfish
3 large shrimp
1 pound tagliolini, packaged or homemade
3 tablespoons butter
2 shallots, peeled and finely diced
3 tablespoons cognac or brandy
1 cup heavy cream
Juice of 1 lemon (about)
Salt and freshly ground white pepper to taste

1. Place the live lobster head down in a large pot of boiling, salted water. Cook for 5 minutes. Remove and refresh in ice water.

2. Add the crayfish to the boiling water the lobster was cooked in, and boil for 2 to 3 minutes. Remove the crayfish and refresh in ice water.

3. Add the shrimp to the boiling lobster water and boil for 2 to 3 minutes. Remove and refresh in ice water.

4. Remove the shells from all the seafood and cut the meat into medium-size cubes. Set aside.

5. Cook the pasta in plenty of boiling, salted water until done "al dente," tender but firm. Strain and refresh in ice water to halt the cooking. Set aside.

6. Heat the butter in a large skillet and sauté the shellfish for 1 minute.

7. Add the shallots and cognac or brandy. Flambé: cook over low heat for 1 minute, until the liquor has warmed. Ignite the liquor, being careful to stand back. Let it flambé till the flame is exhausted,

about 2 minutes. Remove the shellfish and keep warm in a covered plate.

8. Add the cream to the skillet. Over medium heat, reduce by about half to a sauce consistency. Add lemon juice and salt and pepper to taste.

9. Stir in the seafood. Add the tagliolini and stir carefully into the sauce a few times, coating it well.

10. Serve immediately in warm soup plates.

TAGLIOLINI WITH MUSSELS, CLAMS, AND CARROTS

SERVES 6

1 pound tagliolini, packaged or homemade
5 tablespoons olive oil
8 shallots, peeled and thinly sliced
4 garlic cloves, peeled, crushed, and cut in half
30 mussels, rinsed and debearded
1 cup dry white wine
30 clams, rinsed and cleaned
1 large carrot, peeled and finely diced
1/2 cup heavy cream
Juice of 1 lemon (about)
Salt and freshly ground white pepper to taste

1. Cook the pasta in plenty of boiling, salted water until done "al dente," tender but firm. Strain and refresh in ice water to halt the cooking. Set aside.

2. Heat 2 tablespoons of the olive oil in a pot. Add half of the sliced shallots and half of the crushed garlic cloves. Sauté over medium-high heat for 5 minutes.

3. Add the mussels and sauté until they open.

4. Add the wine and enough water to cover the mussels. Boil for 5 minutes.

5. Remove the mussels and add the clams to the boiling stock. When the clams have opened, remove them and reserve the stock.

6. Take the mussel and clam meat out of the shells and set aside. Keep 6 nice mussel shells and 6 nice clamshells for a garnish.

7. Heat the remaining 3 tablespoons olive oil in a large saucepan. Add the remaining shallots and garlic. Sauté briefly.

8. Add the diced carrot and 1/2 cup of the reserved stock. Reduce by half.

9. Add the heavy cream and reduce by about half to a sauce consistency. Season with lemon juice and salt and pepper to taste.

10. Stir in the mussels and clams. Add the pasta and carefully stir it in the sauce a few times to coat it.

11. Serve immediately in 6 warm soup plates. Garnish each portion with a mussel shell and a clamshell.

SEAFOOD TERRINE WITH LOBSTER

SERVES 18

When sliced, this terrine reveals a rich layer of everyone's favorite, lobster, couched in a baked mousse of sole, scallops, cream, and seasonings.

1 pound sea scallops
1 pound lemon sole fillets
1/4 cup heavy cream
1 egg white
Juice of 1 lemon
1 tablespoon tarragon vinegar
Salt and freshly ground white pepper to taste
Butter to grease the terrine
Meat of 2 lobster tails, weighing a total of 1 pound (the
    lobster tails may be purchased already poached, with
    the meat separated)

1. Place the scallops and lemon sole fillets in a food processor. Add the cream, egg white, lemon juice, and vinegar. Puree until the mixture forms a smooth mousse.

2. Press the mousse through a fine sieve, discarding whatever does not pass through. Add salt and white pepper to taste.

3. Preheat the oven to 250° F.

4. Pour half of the puree into a buttered 2-quart earthenware terrine or 13 × 9 × 2-inch loaf pan. Layer the meat of the two lobster tails over this and cover with the remaining puree.

5. Place the terrine in a flat pan filled with hot water and bake for 15 to 20 minutes. Remove from the oven and allow to cool.

6. Place a large serving dish at least the same size as the terrine on top and turn upside down to unmold. Before serving, cut the seafood mold into slices about 3/4 inch wide.

COLD SEAFOOD TERRINE WITH RED
AND GREEN PEPPER SAUCE

SERVES 18

A colorful pepper sauce enhances the flavors and highlights the festive color of the seafood terrine. This appetizer makes a stunning presentation and is sublimely delicious, too.
Wine recommendation: Gumpoldskirchner Pinot Blanc.

2 pounds filleted turbot
Juice of 3 lemons
1 quart heavy cream
4 egg whites
2 teaspoons cognac
2 teaspoons dry vermouth
6 tablespoons finely chopped watercress
Salt and freshly ground white pepper to taste
2 pounds filleted Dover sole
1 teaspoon saffron, soaked in a teaspoon of dry vermouth a
    minimum of 5 minutes, to bring out the color
2 pounds filleted salmon
Butter for the terrine

RED AND GREEN PEPPER SAUCES
6 sweet red peppers, seeded, cored, and finely sliced
6 sweet green peppers, seeded, cored, and finely sliced
2 tablespoons butter
2 teaspoons dry white wine
2 teaspoons dry vermouth
2 teaspoons cognac
3 cups heavy cream
1 cup sour cream
2 teaspoons sherry vinegar
1 teaspoon ground nutmeg
Salt and freshly ground white pepper to taste

1. Place the turbot in a food processor with the juice of 1 lemon, 1¼ cups of the cream, 2 egg whites, 1 teaspoon of the cognac, 1 teaspoon of the vermouth, all of the watercress, and salt and white pepper to taste. Puree until smooth and strain through a fine sieve. Set aside in a bowl.

2. Place the Dover sole in the processor with the juice of 1 lemon, 1¼ cups of the cream, and the remaining 2 egg whites, 1 teaspoon of cognac, and 1 teaspoon of vermouth. Drain the saffron and add it with salt and white pepper to taste. Puree until smooth, strain through a fine sieve, and set aside in a bowl.

3. Place the salmon in the processor with the juice of 1 lemon, 1¼ cups of cream, and salt and white pepper to taste. Puree until smooth, strain through a fine sieve, and set aside in a bowl.

4. Preheat the oven to the lowest possible setting.

5. Butter a 2-quart earthenware terrine and line the bottom and sides with baking parchment. Layer the pink, green, and yellow seafood mousse for a colorful effect. Cover the top of the terrine with baking parchment.

6. Place the terrine in a pan of hot water. Place the pan in the oven and poach for 35 minutes. Remove the terrine from the oven and allow to cool. Unmold by placing a plate of at least the same size as the terrine on top and turn upside down. Peel off the baking parchment.

7. To prepare the sauces: in separate pans, over medium heat, sauté the red and the green peppers in a tablespoon of butter each for 10 minutes.

8. Add 1 teaspoon each of the wine, vermouth, and cognac to each pan. Add 1½ cups of cream to each pan and reduce by half.

9. Separately blend the contents of each pan in a food processor. Strain each through a fine sieve. Set the red and green sauces aside in separate bowls to cool.

10. Stir into each bowl ½ cup of the sour cream and then 1 teaspoon of the sherry vinegar. To each bowl add ½ teaspoon of ground nutmeg and salt and white pepper to taste, and stir.

11. Place 2 tablespoons of each sauce on each plate. Shake the plates to swirl the sauces together for a colorful effect. Serve 2 slices of the seafood terrine over the sauce.

VEAL AND VEGETABLE TERRINE WITH
WATERCRESS SAUCE

SERVES 12

This mousse of ground veal, layered with a mosaic of crisp, particol-
ored vegetables, makes a luscious beginning for dinner or a sophisticated after-theater supper.

1 pound lean ground veal
1 cup heavy cream
2 egg whites
2 tablespoons Madeira
2 tablespoons cognac
Salt and freshly ground white pepper to taste
12 string beans, with both ends snapped off
1/2 medium carrot, peeled and cut into 1/2-inch strips
1/2 medium yellow turnip, peeled and cut into 1/2-inch
    strips
1/2 head cauliflower, cut into small flowerets
2 celery stalks, with any tough strings removed from the
    sides, cut into 1/2-inch strips the same length as the
    carrot strips
Bacon lard for lining the terrine

WATERCRESS SAUCE
5 bunches watercress
1/2 cup heavy cream
1 cup sour cream or 1/2 cup sour cream plus 1/4 cup crème
    fraîche
Juice of 1/2 lemon
Salt and freshly ground white pepper to taste

1. Place the veal, cream, egg whites, Madeira, and cognac in a
food processor and puree to a smooth mousse.
2. Strain the mousse through a fine sieve. Add salt and white
pepper to taste. Refrigerate.

3. Blanch separately the string beans, carrot, turnip, cauliflower, and celery by placing briefly in boiling water and then immediately refresh in ice water. Each vegetable must be blanched and refreshed separately. Keep the vegetables in separate bowls to drain.

4. Preheat the oven to 225° F.

5. Line a 2-quart earthenware terrine with thin slices of bacon lard, pressing tightly. Pour one quarter of the veal mousse into the terrine. Arrange stripes of each vegetable for a colorful effect. Alternate layers of meat and vegetables, ending with meat. *Make sure that the sides and ends of the terrine are covered with meat mousse in order to secure the mold.*

6. Cover the terrine, place it in a pan of hot water, and bake for 35 to 40 minutes.

7. Allow the terrine to cool. Place a plate at least the same size as the terrine on top and turn upside down to unmold. Rap the plate with the inverted terrine sharply on a countertop once to loosen the mold.

8. Rinse and drain the watercress. Reserve 6–10 sprigs for garnish. Place in a food processor and add the heavy cream. Blend to the consistency of a thick sauce. Strain through a fine sieve.

9. Stir in the sour cream. Add the lemon juice and stir. Season with salt and white pepper to taste.

10. First pour some sauce on a plate. Cut a slice of the terrine to reveal the beautiful colors, and place on the green sauce. Garnish with a sprig of watercress.

CHAPTER 2

Soups

Austrians attach great importance to soups, considered the essential beginning of a meal. It is unthinkable to serve a dinner without a good soup, fragrant and fortifying, slowly simmered and prepared with love. The typical everyday Viennese soup is beef bouillon, intensified as a golden consommé, and varied with delicious soup garnishes and dumplings. Bouillon is also the basis for many wonderful thick and creamy soups in the Viennese repertoire. Here are our suggestions for soups to entice the appetite as a separate course or satisfy as a meal in themselves.

BOUILLON
Klare Rindsuppe

MAKES 2 QUARTS

This is our basic soup, used year round in Austria to make consommé and other soups. It is especially fine to come home to on a very cold day. In Austria we serve Klare Rindsuppe decorated with colorful snippings of fresh chive or filled with soup garnishes.

2 pounds beef bones
2 medium onions, unpeeled
1½ pounds beef, rinsed under cold water
½ leek, well washed and trimmed
¼ celery root (celeriac), peeled
2 medium carrots, peeled
1 clove garlic, peeled
Stems of 1 bunch parsley, rinsed
10 black peppercorns
1 bay leaf
Salt to taste

1. Rinse the beef bones under cold water, chop into 3-inch pieces, blanch them in boiling water for 2 minutes, then again rinse in cold water.

2. Cut the unpeeled onions in half. Place the cut sides down on a hot stove burner or over a low flame and allow to char.

3. Place the blanched bones and the beef in a large pot with 5 quarts cold water. Bring to a boil, lower the heat, and simmer, uncovered, for 2 hours, skimming frequently. Remove the meat.

4. Add the charred onions, leek, celery root, carrots, garlic, parsley stems, peppercorns, bay leaf, and salt to taste. Cover and continue simmering for another 2 hours.

5. Strain the bouillon first through a sieve and then through cheesecloth.

6. Refrigerate overnight and skim again for the clearest possible consommé.

CONSOMMÉ
Wiener Kraftsuppe

MAKES 2 QUARTS

This recipe may be followed to further intensify and clarify the bouillon. In Vienna, consommé is considered the perfect soup for convalescence, being both nourishing and digestible. In restaurants the consommé is served alone or with delicious garnishes such as Fritatten, Leberknödel, or Griessnockerln (recipes follow).

1 pound lean ground beef
1 medium carrot, peeled and finely diced
1/4 celery root (celeriac), peeled and finely diced
1/2 bunch parsley, finely chopped
3 egg whites
6 black peppercorns
2 quarts cold Bouillon (see preceding recipe)
Salt to taste

1. Mix the meat, vegetables, egg whites, and enough water so that the mixture is still thick but holds together. Refrigerate for 3 hours.

2. Place this mixture in a pot with the peppercorns. Add the cold bouillon. Bring to a boil, stirring frequently. When the boiling point has been reached, stop stirring, and allow grease to rise to the surface. Simmer the soup for 1½ hours, skimming occasionally.

3. Strain through cheesecloth, discard the solids, season with salt, and bring quickly to a boil.

4. Serve in individual bowls with any of the following traditional garnishes.

TRADITIONAL AUSTRIAN GARNISHES
FOR CONSOMMÉ

FRITATTEN
Pancake Strips

MAKES ENOUGH PANCAKES
FOR 8 SERVINGS OF
CONSOMMÉ

1/2 cup flour
1 pint milk
2 eggs
1/2 bunch parsley, finely chopped
Salt and freshly ground white pepper to taste
Pinch of nutmeg
2 tablespoons butter for frying

1. Mix the flour, milk, and eggs to a smooth consistency. Stir in the parsley and season with salt, pepper, and nutmeg to taste.

2. Heat 1/2 tablespoon of the butter in an omelette pan over medium heat and pour in a very thin layer of batter, sufficient to cover the bottom of the pan. Brown on both sides and cut into thin strips while still warm. Repeat with the remaining batter.

3. Float the Fritatten strips on top of the Consommé (see Index) and serve immediately.

LEBERKNÖDEL
Liver Dumplings

MAKES 8–10 DUMPLINGS,
1 PER SERVING OF
CONSOMMÉ

A healthy and tasty addition to the Consommé. The savory combination of aromatic marjoram and liver makes these dumplings exceptional.

1/2 **pound calf's liver, with skin and sinews removed**
1/2 **cup chopped bacon**
3 **French rolls, soaked in 1/2 cup milk, with all the liquid
    then squeezed out**
1 **medium onion, thinly sliced**
1 **tablespoon salad oil**
2 **eggs**
1 **clove garlic, peeled and finely chopped**
1/2 **bunch parsley, finely chopped**
1/4 **teaspoon dried marjoram**
Salt and freshly ground white pepper to taste
1/2 **cup bread crumbs**
4 **cups Bouillon (see Index)**

1. Grind the liver, bacon, and soaked rolls together. (You can use a food processor.)

2. In a skillet, fry the onion in the oil over medium-high heat until translucent, about 10 minutes.

3. In a large bowl, mix the ground liver mixture with the eggs, onion, garlic, and parsley.

4. Season with the marjoram and salt and pepper to taste. Thicken with the bread crumbs and form balls of equal size.

5. In a saucepan, bring the bouillon to a boil, add the dumplings, reduce the heat, and simmer for 10 minutes.

6. Remove the dumplings and serve afloat the Consommé (see Index).

GRIESSNOCKERLN
Small Semolina Dumplings

MAKES 6–8 DUMPLINGS,
1 PER SERVING OF
CONSOMMÉ

These dumplings are soft and fluffy, cloudlike accents for the consommé, and simple to prepare.

1 egg
4 tablespoons butter, melted
1/2 cup coarse-ground semolina
Salt to taste
3 cups Bouillon (see Index)

1. Beat the egg and butter until frothy. Stir in the semolina and season with salt. Cover and allow to rest 15 minutes.

2. In a saucepan, bring the bouillon to a boil. Form oval dumplings with a spoon and slide them into the bouillon. Reduce the heat and allow to simmer 10 minutes. Remove and quickly refresh in cold water.

3. Serve floating in the Consommé (see Index).

Apricot Fruit Dumplings
topped with Poppy Seeds,
Crumbled Farmer Cheese,
and Sweet Bread Crumbs

*Sweetbreads and Foie Gras
on Seasonal Salad*

Braised Pork Fillet on
Champagne Cabbage

*Veal Steak with Morel
Sauce and Potato
Dumplings (left), and
Quail and Squab Breasts
with Green Figs*

Venison Saddle with Port
Sauce and Black Truffles,
before carving

Mussels with Papaya in a
Pommery Mustard Sauce

Esterhazy Rostbraten
with Potato Dumplings
(Sirloin Steak)

GOULASH SOUP

SERVES 6

The sky is an intense azure. Ice-and-snow-laden branches glisten in the sunshine. On a clear day after a heavy snowfall, the Tyrolean Alps are the place to be. After an exhilarating day on the ski slopes, everyone returns to the wood-paneled lodge, crowded with people looking forward to warming up at the fireside with a spicy goulash soup. Serve this winter stew as a meal in itself, with crusty rolls and good beer. A great way to establish a mood of comfort and community at your table.

Traditionally thought of as a Hungarian dish, goulash is very much a part of Austrian cuisine.

2 tablespoons oil for sautéing
3 medium onions, peeled and diced
2 tablespoons tomato puree
1/4 cup flour
1 tablespoon sweet Hungarian paprika
1 tablespoon red wine vinegar
6 cups Bouillon (see Index)
6 ounces lean beef, cut into 1-inch cubes (3/4–1 cup cubed)
1 garlic clove, peeled and crushed
1/2 teaspoon caraway seeds
1/2 teaspoon dried marjoram
Salt to taste
3 medium potatoes, peeled and cut into 1/2-inch cubes

1. Heat the oil in a skillet and sauté the onions until they are golden brown. Add the tomato puree and remove from the heat.

2. Stir in the flour and then the paprika. Add the vinegar and then the bouillon. Stir well and return to the heat.

3. Bring to a boil and add the meat, garlic, caraway, marjoram, and salt to taste. Allow to boil, uncovered, until the meat is tender.

4. Add the potatoes and continue boiling, uncovered, until they are tender but firm.

5. The goulash should be served while piping hot!

POTATO-LEEK SOUP

SERVES 6

Fine served either hot or chilled, this potato-leek soup is a favorite in Austrian households. A subtle hint of nutmeg is necessary, giving this creamy soup its distinctive flavor. The nutmeg should be barely noticeable and never overpowering.

2 tablespoons oil for sautéing
1 medium onion, finely sliced
1 leek (white portion only), finely sliced
2 tablespoons flour
5 cups Bouillon (see Index)
1 pound potatoes, peeled and finely sliced (new potatoes
    are ideal, but use any red-skinned potato)
1/2 cup heavy cream
2 tablespoons butter
1/8 teaspoon ground nutmeg
Salt and freshly ground white pepper to taste
1/2 bunch parsley, finely chopped
Croutons (sauté a finely cubed roll or slice of white bread
    in butter until golden)

1. Heat the oil in a large saucepan and sauté the onion and leek over medium heat.

2. Stir in the flour and then add the bouillon. Bring to a boil, add the potatoes, and cook until tender, about 25 minutes.

3. Puree the soup in a blender. Return the soup to the saucepan. Add the cream and butter. Heat through over a low flame. Season with the nutmeg and salt and pepper to taste.

4. Serve in individual soup bowls, each portion sprinkled with chopped parsley. Serve the croutons separately.

SOUR CREAM SOUP
Stoss-Suppe

SERVES 6

One of the most memorable experiences a traveler can have is an autumn train ride from Vienna to Graz, capital of Styria, southwest of Vienna. The train winds through densely forested mountains, glorious with the season's colors—a spectacular panorama. Stoss-Suppe originates in this mountainous region. Our Sour Cream Soup is a rendition of this Styrian specialty. Vinegar and caraway seeds add a distinctive depth to this smooth soup.

5 cups Bouillon (see Index)
1 teaspoon caraway seeds
2 cups sour cream
2 tablespoons flour
1 teaspoon red wine vinegar
Salt and freshly ground white pepper to taste
4 tablespoons butter
Croutons (sauté a finely cubed roll or slice of white bread
**   in butter until golden)**

1. In a saucepan, bring the bouillon and caraway seeds to a boil. Blend the sour cream and flour and add to the pot. Stir in smoothly.

2. Simmer, uncovered, over low heat until a soup consistency is reached; this will take about 25 minutes.

3. Stir in the vinegar and season with salt and pepper to taste. Swirl in the butter.

4. Serve in individual bowls, topping with the croutons.

CREAM SOUP WITH HERBS AND SWEETBREAD CUBES

SERVES 6

A noble beginning for an elegant dinner. Abundant fresh basil, tarragon, lemon balm, and sorrel accent this inventive interpretation of a traditional Viennese pairing.

2 tablespoons butter
1/2 onion, thinly sliced
1 leek (white portion only), rinsed very thoroughly and sliced
1 1/2 tablespoons fresh basil leaves, rinsed, patted dry, and finely chopped
1/2 tablespoon fresh lemon balm leaves, rinsed, patted dry, and finely chopped
1/2 tablespoon fresh tarragon leaves, rinsed, patted dry, and finely chopped
1/2 tablespoon fresh sorrel, rinsed, patted dry, and finely chopped
4 tablespoons flour
2 tablespoons red wine vinegar
1 quart heavy cream
4 cups Bouillon (see Index)
1 tablespoon lemon juice
Salt and freshly ground white pepper to taste
2 ounces sweetbreads, cleaned, blanched in boiling water, refreshed in ice water, and cut into 1/2-inch cubes (4 tablespoons cubed)
1/2 bunch parsley, finely chopped

1. Heat the butter in a skillet and sauté the onion and leek over medium heat.

2. Stir in the herbs (except the parsley) and flour and heat through for a minute. Cool with the red wine vinegar.

3. Add the cream and bring to a boil.

4. Add the bouillon, bring to a boil, and reduce to a soup consistency.

5. Season with lemon juice and salt and pepper to taste.

6. Serve in warm soup bowls, over the sweetbread cubes, and
garnished with the parsley.

ASPARAGUS CREAM SOUP

SERVES 6

A soup with finesse to celebrate the spring.

1¹/₂ pounds green asparagus, trimmed
¹/₄ teaspoon salt
3 pints Chicken Stock (see Index)
6 tablespoons butter
4 tablespoons flour
Salt and freshly ground white pepper to taste
¹/₈ teaspoon ground nutmeg
1¹/₂ cups heavy cream
2 egg yolks
¹/₂ bunch parsley, finely chopped

1. Boil the asparagus in 2 cups water with ¹/₄ teaspoon salt added, until tender. Lift the asparagus out of the pot and drain. Reserve the cooking water. Cut the tips off the asparagus and reserve for garnishing. Cut the asparagus stems into small pieces.

2. Puree the asparagus pieces in a blender or food processor and press through a sieve.

3. In a large saucepan, mix the pureed asparagus with the salted cooking water. Add the chicken stock. Bring to a boil and allow to reduce for 15 minutes.

4. Prepare a white roux by melting the butter in a saucepan and stirring in the flour.

5. Ladle ¹/₄ cup of the hot stock into the roux and blend thoroughly. Pour this mixture back into the soup, whisking thoroughly. Bring to a boil and reduce to a smooth consistency.

6. Remove the soup from the heat. Season with salt, pepper, and nutmeg to taste. Whisk in the cream and egg yolks.

7. Return to the heat and bring quickly to a boil.

8. Serve in warm soup bowls, garnished with chopped parsley and the asparagus tips.

CHAPTER 3

Salads and Salad Dressings

Mixed leaf salads and impeccable vegetables should enter into harmonies of color, texture, and flavor. Give your fantasy free rein. An imaginatively prepared salad, utilizing the freshest seasonal produce, refreshes and invigorates the palate. It is a pleasurable experience to wander a country garden or city market in quest of the choicest salad ingredients and then dress them with a balanced vinaigrette.

Our basic vinaigrette is one part vinegar or lemon juice to two parts salad oil. A teaspoon of mustard, crushed garlic, or a fragrant mixture of fresh herbs may of course be added. The following are popular salad dressings, frequently used in Viennese cuisine. Note that the Viennese Vinaigrette includes sugar, which intensifies the flavor of tomatoes in a remarkable way.

VIENNESE VINAIGRETTE

1 part white wine vinegar mixed with an equal amount of water
1/2 teaspoon powdered sugar per cup of liquid
Salt and freshly ground black pepper to taste
2 parts salad oil

Blend well and serve.

LEMON DRESSING

1 part fresh lemon juice
Salt and freshly ground white pepper to taste
Pinch of sugar
2 parts salad oil

Blend well. Serve with leaf salads.

EGG DRESSING FOR VEGETABLE SALADS

MAKES ABOUT 1³/4 CUPS

Especially fine with crudités.

1/2 cup vinegar
1 teaspoon Dijon-style mustard
Salt and freshly ground black pepper to taste
2 sieved hard-boiled egg yolks
1 cup oil

Blend well and serve.

SOUR CREAM DRESSING

MAKES ABOUT 1¹/4 CUPS

Dill, with its anise overtone, adds great flavor to mixed salads.

2 tablespoons lemon juice
Salt and freshly ground white pepper to taste
1 tablespoon chopped fresh dill
1 cup sour cream

Blend well and serve.

YOGURT DRESSING

MAKES ABOUT 1¼ CUPS

A zesty accent for mixed salads.

2 tablespoons lemon juice
Salt and freshly ground white pepper to taste
1 tablespoon chopped fresh dill
1 cup yogurt

Blend well and serve.

VIENNESE TOMATO SALAD

SERVES 6

The tomatoes for this salad most be ripe but firm. The warm ruby glow of vine-ripened tomatoes pairs beautifully with a sprinkling of dark green chives fresh from your herb garden. This Viennese standard is appropriate for all meat and poultry dishes.

12 medium, ripe tomatoes
1 cup Viennese Vinaigrette (see Index)
1 large onion, sliced
½ bunch chives, minced

1. Dip the tomatoes in boiling water for 5 seconds, refresh in ice water, then peel. Cut into slices or wedges.
2. Pour the vinaigrette into a salad bowl. Mix in the sliced onion and half of the chives.
3. Add the tomato slices and fold carefully.
4. Arrange attractively on individual salad plates and sprinkle with the remaining chives.

VIENNESE CUCUMBER SALAD

SERVES 6

Garlic adds depth to this salad, a perfect accompaniment for pork dishes or any fried food.

2 medium cucumbers, peeled and thinly sliced
1/2 teaspoon salt
3 cloves garlic, peeled and crushed
3 tablespoons red wine vinegar
1/2 teaspoon sweet Hungarian paprika, or to taste
6 tablespoons olive oil

1. Place the cucumber slices in a salad bowl and sprinkle with salt. Add the garlic, cover the bowl, and allow to rest about 1/2 hour.
2. Add the vinegar, 1 tablespoon cold water, and paprika to taste. Stir well, add the oil, and stir again.
3. Since the Viennese Cucumber Salad has a liquid consistency, serve it in small salad bowls, garnished with a pinch of paprika.

VIENNESE POTATO SALAD

SERVES 6

Austrians love potatoes. If they are not served as a side dish, this potato salad would appear on the table. Use paprika and fresh chives as a colorful and delicious garnish for this salad.

2 pounds red-skinned potatoes
1 cup Viennese Vinaigrette (see Index)
1 large onion, chopped
1 bunch chives, chopped
Salt and freshly ground black pepper to taste
6 large green lettuce leaves
Sweet Hungarian paprika

1. Boil the potatoes but do not overcook—they should still be firm. Allow to cool, then peel and cut into medium slices.

2. Pour the Viennese Vinaigrette into a salad bowl. Add the chopped onion and most of the chives (reserve 1 tablespoon for garnishing). Stir well. Season with salt and black pepper to taste.

3. Add the potatoes, stir to coat, and allow to rest 15 minutes.

4. Serve the salad on the lettuce leaves on individual plates. Garnish with the remaining chives and a sprinkling of paprika.

VIENNESE POTATO SALAD WITH MAYONNAISE

SERVES 6

Perfect for a picnic; excellent with chicken and cold cuts. We suggest using red-skinned potatoes, which are firm when sliced, adapting well to salads.

2 pounds potatoes (preferably red-skinned)
2 tablespoons red wine vinegar
5 tablespoons mayonnaise
2 cornichons, cubed
Salt and freshly ground white pepper to taste
1 cornichon, thinly sliced

1. Boil the potatoes only until still firm. Allow them to cool, and then peel and cut into medium slices.

2. Pour the vinegar and 1 tablespoon water into a large bowl. Add the potatoes and stir well. Allow to rest 15 minutes, stirring frequently.

3. Mix the mayonnaise and cubed cornichons in a separate large bowl.

4. Add the potatoes, mix well, and season with salt and white pepper.

5. Arrange on individual salad plates and garnish with the sliced cornichon.

CUCUMBER SALAD WITH NEW POTATOES

SERVES 6

A refreshing variation on the classic Viennese Cucumber Salad, this is also good with fried foods and pork.

1 pound new potatoes
1 medium cucumber
4 tablespoons red wine vinegar
1 teaspoon salt
Freshly ground black pepper to taste
2 cloves garlic, peeled and crushed
6 tablespoons olive oil
Sweet Hungarian paprika

1. Boil the potatoes, taking care not to overcook them—they should still be firm. Drain the potatoes, allow them to cool, and cut them into medium slices.

2. Peel and thinly slice the cucumber, reserving 6 medium slices unpeeled for garnishing.

3. Pour 2 tablespoons of the vinegar and 1 tablespoon water in a salad bowl. Add the salt, some freshly ground black pepper, and the garlic. Add the cucumber and potatoes, stir well, and marinate for 15 minutes.

4. Add the remaining 2 tablespoons vinegar and the oil. Mix well.

5. Place the unpeeled cucumber slices on a paper towel and sprinkle with paprika.

6. Distribute the salad on chilled plates and garnish with the paprika-cucumber slices.

CHAPTER 4

Seafood

V aried, low in calories, and nutritious, seafood is undeniably granted pride of place in contemporary cuisine. Our stellar chef, Andreas Kisler, first developed a love of fish preparations while studying at La Marée, one of the finest seafood restaurants in Paris. Young and innovative, Andy has developed seafood recipes that are subtle and distinctly sophisticated.

LEMON SOLE IN A LEEK CREAM

SERVES 6

A satiny leek cream enhances the delicate flavor of lemon sole in a unique way. Serve this dish with a simple green salad and boiled new potatoes, drizzled with melted butter and sprinkled with fresh parsley. A well-chilled dry white wine is a fine accompaniment. We recommend Grinzinger Chardonnay.

1/2 cup plus 2 tablespoons clarified butter
3 leeks (white portion only), rinsed thoroughly; 2 thinly
    sliced, and 1 thinly sliced lengthwise à la julienne and
    kept separately from the other 2
6 shallots, peeled and finely diced
1/3 cup Fish Stock (see Index)
1/4 cup dry vermouth
1/4 cup dry white wine
1 cup heavy cream
Juice of 1 lemon
Salt and freshly ground white pepper to taste
6 (6-ounce) lemon sole fillets
Flour for the fish

1. Heat 1/4 cup of the clarified butter in a skillet over low heat. Add the sliced leeks and allow to sweat.

2. Add the shallots and continue cooking until transparent.

3. Add the fish stock, vermouth, and white wine. Bring to a very slow boil. Overcook the leek to make sure it is quite soft. This should take about 10 minutes. When the leek is soft, allow the mixture to cool and puree in a blender to a smooth consistency.

4. Transfer the mixture to a saucepan. Add the cream and cook over medium heat until reduced to a sauce consistency. Stir in the lemon juice and season with salt and pepper to taste. Set aside.

5. Dip one side of each lemon sole fillet in flour and shake off the excess. Heat 1/4 cup of the clarified butter in a large skillet over medium-high heat. Fry the fish first on the floured side until golden, then turn and fry on the other side until golden outside and slightly

pink inside. Remove and keep the fish warm on a covered plate.

6. Add 2 tablespoons clarified butter to the skillet and sauté the julienned leek over medium heat for 3 to 4 minutes. Add a few tablespoons of water and allow the leek to blanch.

7. Pour the sauce on 6 warm plates. Arrange the fish over the sauce and garnish with the julienned leek.

ST. PIERRE WITH FENNEL MOUSSE AU GRATIN

SERVES 6

Check your specialty market for St. Pierre, an Atlantic fish widely known in France and increasingly popular in the United States. (It is also called John Dory.) The flavor is similar to that of sole, but its meat is wonderfully firm. We give St. Pierre regal treatment, crowning it with a rich and golden fennel mousse.

Wine recommendation: Sauvignon Blanc by Klosterkeller Siegendorf.

1/2 cup plus 2 tablespoons clarified butter
2 medium fennel heads, thinly sliced (reserve the green
    parts for garnishing)
1 cup heavy cream
2 egg yolks, beaten
3 whole St. Pierre fish, with skin and bones removed, cut
    into 12 fillets
Flour for the fish
4 shallots, peeled and finely diced
2 tablespoons sherry vinegar
1/3 cup dry red wine
4 tablespoons Fish Stock (see Index)
6 tablespoons butter
Juice of 1 lemon
Salt and freshly ground white pepper to taste

1. Heat 1/4 cup of the clarified butter in a skillet and sauté the fennel over medium heat. Cover the fennel with water and cook until soft. Strain off the water. Place the fennel in a food processor, puree, and strain through a fine sieve.

2. Place the puree in a saucepan, add 1/3 cup of the cream, and reduce by half. Lower the heat. Slowly stir in the 2 egg yolks, making sure that the mixture does not boil. Set aside.

3. Dip one side of each fish fillet in flour and shake off the excess. Heat 1/4 cup of the clarified butter in a skillet and sauté the fish over medium-high heat, first on the floured side until golden,

and then on the other side until golden. Remove the fish and keep warm on a covered plate.

4. Heat 2 tablespoons clarified butter and sauté the shallots until golden.

5. Preheat the broiler.

6. Add the sherry vinegar, red wine, and fish stock, and reduce almost all of the liquid. Add the remaining 2/3 cup cream and reduce to a sauce consistency. Swirl in the butter. Stir in the lemon juice and season with salt and pepper to taste.

7. Spread the fennel mousse over the St. Pierre fillets and run under the preheated broiler until browned and hot inside.

8. Place the fish on 6 warm plates, surround with the sauce, and garnish with the fennel greens.

BROOK TROUT AU BLEU

SERVES 6

Austrians especially prize the swiftly moving trout caught fresh from clear mountain streams and quickly poached to achieve the characteristic blue color. We find that dill and fennel seed give a distinctive perfume to the classic court bouillon used for poaching. Our trout is drenched with brown butter and decorated with crispy fried parsley and bright wedges of lemon. A leaf salad is all that is needed to complete this simple feast for the nature lover. Uncork a well-chilled Riesling Spätlese.

6 (12-ounce) fresh trout, with insides removed but left whole*

8 tablespoons butter

Oil for frying the parsley

1 bunch curly parsley

3 lemons, cut in wedges, with seeds removed

COURT BOUILLON

1 quart Fish Stock (see Index)

1 cup dry white wine

1/2 cup white vinegar

1 medium carrot, peeled and sliced

1 medium celery stalk, sliced

1 medium onion, sliced

1 leak (white portion only), well rinsed and sliced

1 teaspoon dillseed

1 teaspoon fennel seeds

1 bay leaf

1 teaspoon white peppercorns

1/2 tablespoon salt

1. Place all of the ingredients for the court bouillon in a pot and bring to a boil. Lower the flame, add the trout, and simmer briefly until the trout turn blue and the eyes shrink to button size.

* Note that a trout that has been frozen will not turn blue when poached.

2. Carefully remove the trout from the stock. Dry on paper towels and place on 6 warm plates.

3. Heat the butter in a skillet over medium heat until it is light brown but not burned.

4. While the butter is browning, heat some oil in another skillet and fry the parsley over high heat until it is crisp but still green, about 2 to 3 minutes.

5. Pour the browned butter over the trout and garnish with the fried parsley and lemon wedges.

COHO BABY SALMON WITH GLAZED GRAPES

SERVES 6

A colorful port and grape sauce transforms the finely textured baby salmon into a festive dish. Serve with rice and a leaf salad.

1/2 cup plus 2 tablespoons grape-seed oil, or, if not available, clarified butter
6 (10-ounce) Coho baby salmon, filleted
4 shallots, peeled and finely diced
3/4 cup seedless red grapes
3/4 cup seedless white grapes
2 tablespoons red wine vinegar
1/4 cup port wine
1/4 cup Fish Stock (see Index)
1/2 cup heavy cream
Juice of 1 lemon
Salt and freshly ground white pepper to taste
4 tablespoons butter
2 tablespoons clarified butter
1 tablespoon sugar

1. Heat 1/2 cup of the grape-seed oil in a skillet and sauté the salmon over medium-high heat for 2 to 3 minutes on each side. The fish should remain slightly pink inside. Remove the fish and keep warm on a covered plate.

2. Heat the remaining 2 tablespoons grape-seed oil in the same skillet and sauté the shallots until golden.

3. Add half of the red and half of the white grapes. Sauté over medium heat for not more than 2 minutes.

4. Add the vinegar and reduce almost all of the liquid.

5. Add the port and reduce by half.

6. Add stock (with no further reducing). Blend all of the above in a food processor or blender and strain through a fine sieve to remove all the grape skin.

7. Place the mixture in a pan, add the cream, and reduce to a sauce consistency over medium heat. Stir in the lemon juice

and season with salt and pepper to taste. Swirl in the 4 tablespoons of butter.

8. Heat 2 tablespoons clarified butter in another pan and sauté the remaining grapes over medium heat for not more than 2 minutes. Add the sugar and heat through a moment.

9. Pour the sauce on 6 warm plates and arrange the salmon over the sauce. Garnish the fish with the glazed grapes.

PIKE QUENELLES IN DILL SAUCE

SERVES 6

The meat of the pike is sweet and firm, ideally suited for forming these fluffy dumplings. The fish is so low in calories that it makes up for the cream that we use in the smooth binding of dill, an aromatic emphasis for the fish. Serve with a julienne of seasonal vegetables. A dry white wine is the suitable accompaniment.

If pike is not available, we suggest using lemon sole or, less expensively, flounder.

1 pound pike fillets
2 cups heavy cream
2 egg whites
Juice of 1 lemon
4 cups Fish Stock (see Index)
1 cup dry white wine
3 tablespoons clarified butter
6 shallots, peeled and finely diced
1/2 bunch fresh dillweed, chopped without stems (reserve a
**   little finely chopped dill for garnish)**
4 tablespoons white vinegar
6 tablespoons butter
1/4 cup whipped cream
Pinch of ground nutmeg
Salt and freshly ground white pepper to taste

1. Place the pike, 1 cup of the cream, the egg whites, and lemon juice in a food processor and puree until smooth. Strain through a fine sieve.

2. Form 18 quenelles by placing 1 tablespoon of fish mixture in the palm of your hand. Smooth it into an oval. Scoop up the fish mixture with a tablespoon and gently place it on a plate. Repeat to form all the quenelles.

3. Place the fish stock and white wine in a large pot. Heat to a simmer, add all the quenelles, and poach until tender, approximately 5 minutes. Remove the quenelles and keep warm on a covered plate. Reserve the poaching liquid.

4. Heat the clarified butter in a skillet and sauté the shallots over medium heat until golden. Add the dillweed and sauté for 1 minute. Pour in the poaching liquid (there should be about 3 cups) and reduce by half. Add the remaining cup of cream and reduce to a sauce consistency. Add the vinegar. Swirl in the 6 tablespoons of butter and then strain the sauce into another pan.

5. Carefully fold in the whipped cream and finish the sauce with ground nutmeg and salt and pepper to taste.

6. Place the quenelles on 6 warm plates and spoon sauce over them. Garnish with the chopped dill.

RED SNAPPER IN CITRUS SAUCE WITH JULIENNE OF VEGETABLES

The combination of orange, lemon, and lime juice with dry vermouth gives a zesty, tropical bouquet to the red snapper. Served with white rice, this is great fare for summer dining. Wine recommendation: a Chablis by Joseph Drouhin.

1 cup dry white wine
1 cup dry vermouth
1 bay leaf
6 white peppercorns
1 medium carrot, cut à la julienne, into thin strips
1 fennel root, cut à la julienne
1 celery root (celeriac), cut à la julienne
Juice of 2 lemons
Juice of 2 limes
Juice of 1 orange
1 cup heavy cream
2 Belgian endives, cut à la julienne
2 tablespoons butter
2 tablespoons Dijon mustard
Salt and freshly ground white pepper to taste
1/4 cup clarified butter
6 (6-ounce) fillets of red snapper
Flour for the fish

1. Pour 3 cups of water and the white wine and vermouth into a medium-sized pot, and add the bay leaf and peppercorns. Bring to a boil and then strain off the bay leaf and peppercorns. Return to a boil and cook the carrot, fennel, and celery root separately until tender. When each vegetable is done, remove from the stock, refresh in ice water, and set aside separately. Reserve the stock.

2. Raise the flame under the stock. Add all of the citrus juices and the cream. Reduce to a sauce consistency. Add the blanched vegetables. Bring to a boil and immediately remove from the flame.

3. Add the endive. Swirl in the butter and then swirl in the mustard. Season with salt and pepper to taste. Set aside and keep warm on the stove top. To prevent the mustard from clumping, do not allow the sauce to cook.

4. Heat the clarified butter in a skillet. Dip the meat side of each fish fillet in the flour. Briefly fry the fish on the skinless side for 2 to 3 minutes and then turn and fry on the skin side until crisp and tender.

5. Place the fish on 6 warm plates and cover with the vegetable sauce.

LANGOUSTINES IN A PERNOD-GINGER SAUCE

SERVES 6

Pungent ginger is a favorite in Chinese seafood preparations. Here lime-soaked ginger marries with the distinctive flavor of anisette to create an innovative meeting of East and West. These langoustines should be served alone, elegantly garnished with claws and lime sections. The sauce is also delicious with lobster if you can't find langoustines.

2 tablespoons Rose's unsweetened lime juice
1 tablespoon very finely diced fresh ginger root
1 leek (white portion only), finely diced
1 medium carrot, peeled and finely diced
1 medium yellow turnip, peeled and finely diced (about 3
    cups diced)
18 langoustines, not larger than 3 ounces each, or 18 jumbo
    shrimp
1/4 cup dry white wine
1/4 cup Pernod
1 cup heavy cream
1/4 cup clarified butter for frying
Salt and freshly ground white pepper to taste
3 limes, cut in wedges, for garnishing

1. Combine the Rose's lime juice and the ginger cubes. Set aside.

2. Bring 1 quart of water to a boil in a medium pot. Add the cubed vegetables and the langoustines. Cook for 2 minutes over low heat. Remove the langoustines and refresh in ice water. Remove the tails from the body and take out the tail meat. Set aside. Twist off the claws and reserve for a garnish.

3. Remove the vegetables from the stock and set aside. Reserve 1/4 cup of the stock.

4. Pour the reserved stock into a saucepan. Add the white wine and Pernod. Reduce by half. Add the ginger and half of the lime

juice it was soaking in. Add the cream and reduce to a sauce consistency. Swirl in the vegetables.

5. Heat the clarified butter in a skillet. Sauté the langoustine meat for 2 to 3 minutes over high heat. Season with salt and pepper to taste.

6. Place langoustine meat in the center of each warm plate with a set of claws above and below it, pincers facing in opposite directions. Place lime sections between the pincers. Cover the meat with the ginger sauce.

SOFT-SHELL CRABS WITH ALMOND SAUCE

SERVES 6

This light, delicious dish is perfect for late-night suppers—or halve the recipe and serve it as an elegant appetizer. The almond sauce gives this traditional American fare a touch of Austrian flavor.

12 soft-shell crabs
Flour for dipping
Salt and freshly ground white pepper to taste
1/2 cup butter
Toasted almond slivers for garnish

ALMOND SAUCE
1 tablespoon butter
1/2 cup almonds, blanched and finely ground
2 tablespoons Amaretto liqueur
4 tablespoons white wine
4 tablespoons Fish Stock (see Index) or bottled clam juice
Juice of 1 lemon
Juice of 1/2 grapefruit
1/4 cup plain yogurt
1/2 cup sour cream
Salt and freshly ground white pepper to taste

1. Rinse the crabs and pat dry with paper towels. Season the flour with salt and pepper. Roll each crab in the flour, shake off the excess, and set aside.

2. Begin the almond sauce: melt the tablespoon of butter in a saucepan over low heat. Add the ground almonds and sauté for 5 minutes. Add the Amaretto, wine, fish stock, and lemon and grapefruit juices and stir well. Bring to a boil over high heat and continue boiling for 2 to 3 minutes to allow the alcohol to evaporate. Set aside to cool.

3. Melt the 1/2 cup of butter in a large skillet over medium heat. Add the crabs to the skillet and sauté for 2 to 3 minutes on each

side, until golden brown. If the crabs are small, you can sauté them all at once; otherwise, do 6 at a time. Remove the crabs to a covered platter and keep warm.

4. Finish the almond sauce: mix the yogurt and sour cream in a large bowl. When the almond sauce has reached room temperature, slowly stir it into the yogurt mixture. Season with salt and pepper to taste.

5. Spoon some sauce on each plate and top with 2 crabs. Sprinkle with toasted almonds.

STRIPED BASS STUFFED WITH
FENNEL, WITH A LITTLENECK CLAM SAUCE

SERVES 6

The versatility of seafood is appreciated the world over. This is a recipe contributed by Peter Moser, master chef at the Palais Schwarzenberg, one of Vienna's most elegant restaurants. In the midst of the busy capital, this baroque palace and its garden are a magic setting for culinary adventure. Serve this impressive stuffed fish with a simple accompaniment, buttered new potatoes.

6 thick 8-ounce fillets of striped bass
2 pounds littleneck clams, cleaned
1 1/8 cups dry white wine
6 teaspoons beef marrow
3/4 cup clarified butter for frying
1 head fennel, thinly sliced (reserve the leaves from the
    fennel head for garnishing)
Pinch of fennel seed
6 tablespoons dry vermouth
1/2 cup Brown Veal Stock (see Index)
6 slices white bread, with crusts removed, cut into 1/2-inch
    cubes
3 egg yolks
2 shallots, peeled and thinly sliced
1 clove garlic, peeled and crushed
1 cup heavy cream
3 tablespoons cognac
Flour for the fish
Juice of 1 lemon
Salt and freshly ground white pepper to taste

1. Lay the striped bass fillets on a flat surface and make an incision lengthwise on the top of each fillet, holding your knife at an angle. This will make a flap under which you can place the stuffing.

2. Boil the clams in 3 cups of water and 1 cup white wine until the shells open. Refresh in ice water and remove the clam meat from the shells. Reserve the meat and discard the shells.

3. Blanch the marrow briefly in boiling water, refresh in ice water, and dice.

4. Heat 1/4 cup of the clarified butter in a skillet over medium-high heat and sauté the fennel slices and fennel seed for 8 to 10 minutes. The fennel should be soft but not browned. Add the vermouth and veal stock. Allow to reduce over medium heat for 10 minutes.

5. With your hands, mix the bread cubes and marrow into a mass. Add this to the fennel. Stir to mix.

6. Remove the skillet from the heat. Slowly whisk in the 3 egg yolks. Set aside to cool.

7. Heat 1/4 cup of the clarified butter in a skillet and sauté the shallots and garlic over medium heat for 4 to 5 minutes. Add the clam meat and the remaining 1/8 cup white wine. Stir in the cream and bring to a very slow boil. While it is boiling, add the cognac. Continue boiling until a sauce consistency is reached.

8. While the sauce is boiling, place some fennel stuffing in each fish fillet and seal the fillet with a toothpick. Dip the fish on the stuffed side in some flour.

9. Heat the remaining 1/4 cup clarified butter in a skillet and fry the fish on the floured side over medium-high heat until golden. Turn and fry on the other side until golden. Remove and keep warm on a covered plate.

10. Pour the sauce into the skillet in which the fish has been fried. Stir in the lemon juice and season with salt and pepper to taste.

11. Pour the clam sauce onto 6 warm plates. Place the stuffed fish fillets over the sauce, remove the toothpicks, and garnish with the reserved fennel leaves.

MEDALLIONS OF LOBSTER IN A DILL-CUCUMBER SAUCE WITH CHICKEN MOUSSE QUENELLES

SERVES 6

A rich but light preparation for an important dinner: lobster medallions luxuriously laden with claw meat, delicately complemented by a refreshing cucumber sauce. Garnished with lovely quenelles, this is a seductive dining experience. Accompany the lobster with an attractive julienne of vegetables. The joyous note of champagne should not be forgotten.

2 (3-pound) lobsters or 1 (6-pound) lobster
4 boneless and skinless whole chicken breasts
3 eggs
1¹/₄ cups heavy cream
Juice of 1 lemon
Salt and freshly ground white pepper to taste
2 medium cucumbers, peeled, with seeds removed, and
    diced
¹/₄ cup dry white wine
¹/₂ bunch fresh dillweed, finely chopped
1 tablespoon sherry vinegar
2 garlic cloves, pureed in a food processor with 5
    tablespoons olive oil

1. Cook the lobsters in boiling water for 10 to 12 minutes. Reserve *all* of the resulting stock and separate ¹/₂ cup of it for use in the sauce. Remove the tail meat from the lobsters and cut into 5 medallions, about 1 inch thick, per person. Set aside. Remove the meat from the claws and cut in half lengthwise. Set aside separately.

2. Puree the chicken breasts, eggs, ¹/₂ cup of the heavy cream, and the lemon juice in a food processor until smooth. Strain through a fine sieve into a bowl. Season with salt and pepper to taste. Place the bowl in a larger bowl filled with ice and chill for 1 hour.

3. Place 1 teaspoon of the fish mixture in the palm of your hand. Smooth it into an oval. Scoop up the mixture with another teaspoon and gently place it on a plate. Repeat to form all the quenelles.

4. Reheat the reserved lobster stock (less the 1/2 cup for the sauce) to a simmer and gently add the quenelles. Poach in the simmering stock until tender, about 5 minutes. Remove the quenelles carefully with a slotted spoon and set aside on a covered plate.

5. Blanch the cucumber cubes briefly in boiling salted water. Strain and then liquefy in a blender. Set aside.

6. Pour the remaining 3/4 cup heavy cream, the white wine, and the 1/2 cup reserved lobster stock into a pan. Cook over a medium flame until reduced by half, about 8 to 10 minutes. Add the liquefied cucumber and continue reducing to a sauce consistency, about 8 to 10 minutes. Finish the sauce with the chopped dill and sherry vinegar. Season with salt and pepper to taste.

7. While the sauce is reducing, heat the garlic oil in a skillet and briefly reheat the lobster medallions. Set aside on a covered plate. Briefly reheat the claw meat and set aside separately.

8. Pour the cucumber sauce onto 6 warm plates. Place the 5 lobster medallions for each serving over the sauce and top them with claw meat. Arrange 3 quenelles on each plate.

SALMON STEAK IN PUFF PASTRY
WITH A SORREL SAUCE

SERVES 6

A study in the elegant combination of texture and flavor. A delicate golden case of puff pastry enfolds moist pink salmon. The whole is eloquently enhanced with the bright green color and lemony tartness of sorrel. Serve with boiled new potatoes and an array of seasonal vegetables. This is a dish that merits a festive champagne.

16 ounces puff pastry (readymade is acceptable)
2¹/₂ pounds fresh salmon, cut into 6 steaks, with skin and bones removed, and sprinkled with salt and pepper
2 egg yolks, beaten with 2 tablespoons water
¹/₂ cup plus 2 tablespoons clarified butter
4 shallots, peeled and finely sliced
1 bunch fresh sorrel, sliced in 1¹/₄-inch-thick strips
¹/₄ cup red wine vinegar
¹/₄ cup dry white wine
¹/₂ cup Fish Stock (see Index)
¹/₂ cup heavy cream
Juice of 1 lemon
Salt and freshly ground white pepper to taste

1. Preheat the oven to 400° F.

2. Roll the puff pastry into 12 squares; 6 squares should be the size of the fish steaks and the other 6 should be slightly larger on each side, to overlap.

2. Place the salmon on the small squares of pastry. Brush the sides of the squares with the beaten egg yolks. Cover with the larger pastry squares and then press to seal. Brush the top of the pastry with the egg yolks.

3. Heat ¹/₂ cup of the clarified butter in an ovenproof skillet. Place the salmon in pastry in the skillet and fry over medium heat for 5 minutes on the bottom side only. Transfer to the preheated oven and bake for 8 to 10 minutes. Remove the pastry packets and keep warm on a covered plate.

4. Heat 2 tablespoons of the clarified butter in a saucepan. Sauté the shallots over medium heat until golden. Add half of the sorrel strips and sauté briefly. Add the red wine vinegar, white wine, and fish stock. Cook over medium heat for 5 minutes, or until reduced by half. Add the cream and continue cooking 5 to 7 minutes, until reduced to a sauce consistency.

5. Strain the sauce into a second pan. Stir in the lemon juice and season with salt and pepper to taste.

6. Pour the sorrel sauce onto 6 warm plates and place the salmon in pastry over the sauce. Arrange the remaining, uncooked sorrel around the pastry.

SALMON FILLETS WITH A SHRIMP RAGOUT

SERVES 6

Garlic adds exciting flavor to this dish contributed by Franz Sam, executive chef at the Fledermaus Café. Serve this sophisticated combination of salmon and shrimp with boiled new potatoes and seasonal vegetables.

2 pounds fresh salmon, with skin and bones removed, cut into 18 equal fillets
White bread crumbs for breading
1/4 cup olive oil for frying
18 medium-sized fresh shrimp, peeled and deveined, cut into 1-inch pieces
4 garlic cloves, peeled and ground in a processor with 2 tablespoons olive oil
4 shallots, finely chopped
1/4 cup dry white wine
1/4 cup Fish Stock (see Index)
1/4 cup heavy cream
6 medium mushroom caps, cut in half
Juice of 1 lemon
Salt and freshly ground white pepper
1/2 bunch parsley, finely chopped

1. Dip the salmon fillets in the white bread crumbs and shake off any excess. Heat the olive oil in a skillet and sauté the fillets over medium-high heat for 2 to 3 minutes until they are golden outside and pink inside. Remove the fillets and keep warm on a covered plate.

2. Sauté the shrimp in the garlic oil. Add the shallots and sauté until golden. Remove the shrimp and shallots and set aside.

3. Add the white wine and the stock to the skillet. Reduce by half. Add the cream and reduce to a sauce consistency. Add the mushrooms and allow to simmer for 1 minute. Stir in the lemon juice, shrimp, and shallots. Season with salt and pepper to taste.

4. Pour the ragout sauce on 6 warm plates and place the fillets over the ragout. Garnish with the chopped parsley.

CHAPTER 5

Veal and Calf's Liver

P earlescent, tender, and free of fat, veal is healthy yet delicate fare, more digestible than beef or pork, and simple to prepare. The subtle flavor of this meat makes it ideally suited for combination with a limitless variety of sauces and seasonings. Viennese cuisine is particularly renowned for its Schnitzel preparations, veal cutlets as delicious as they are quick and easy to prepare. Here we offer several beloved Austrian standards, as well as our own sophisticated variations.

NATURSCHNITZEL

SERVES 6

A flawless delight for the purist. The simple sauce of clear broth and veal stock emphasizes the natural delicacy of the cutlets. We recommend serving the Naturschnitzel with the rice of your choice, such as pressed white rice or Mushroom Rice (see Index). A good wine to drink with many veal dishes is a light Austrian Pinot Blanc.

12 (3½-ounce) cutlets from the top round of veal
Flour
Clarified butter for frying
½ cup dry white wine for degreasing
⅓ cup Consommé (see Index)
½ cup Brown Veal Stock (see Index)
4 tablespoons butter
Salt and freshly ground white pepper to taste

1. Pound the cutlets and make 2 incisions in the edge of each to prevent shrinkage.

2. Dip one side of each cutlet in some flour and shake off the excess. Heat ¼ cup clarified butter in a skillet and sauté several cutlets on the floured side until golden outside but still pink inside, about 2 to 3 minutes. Turn and fry 2 to 3 minutes more on the other side. Add clarified butter as needed for frying the rest of the cutlets. Remove and keep warm on a covered plate.

3. Degrease the skillet by adding the white wine. Add the consommé and reduce by half. Add the veal stock and again reduce by half. Swirl in the butter. Season with salt and pepper to taste. Pour any veal juices from the covered plate into the sauce and heat through.

4. Place 2 cutlets on one side of each individual plate and cover with sauce.

PAPRIKASCHNITZEL

SERVES 6

Smoked bacon and bright paprika give juicy veal cutlets a dramatic accent to round out this classic dish. Serve the mildly spicy Paprikaschnitzel with Spaetzle (see Index) or buttered noodles.

12 (3 1/2-ounce) cutlets from the top round of veal
2 tablespoons finely diced smoked bacon
2 medium onions, finely diced
2 tablespoons sweet Hungarian paprika
Dash of white vinegar
1/3 cup Consommé (see Index)
1/2 cup heavy cream
Juice of 1 lemon
Salt and freshly ground white pepper to taste
Clarified butter for frying
Flour
1/3 cup dry white wine

1. Pound the cutlets and make 2 incisions in the edge of each to prevent shrinkage.

2. Sauté the smoked bacon over medium heat, add the onions, and sauté until golden. Add the paprika and sauté 2 to 3 minutes. (If the paprika is allowed to sauté too long, it has a bitter taste.) Add the vinegar and consommé. Reduce almost all of the liquid. Add the cream and reduce to a sauce consistency. Add the lemon juice and salt and pepper to taste.

3. Heat 1/4 cup clarified butter in another skillet. Dip one side of each cutlet in some flour and shake off the excess. Fry the cutlets on the floured side over medium-high heat until golden, about 2 to 3 minutes. Turn and fry on the other side until golden. Remove and keep warm on a covered plate.

4. Degrease the pan by wiping out with a paper towel. Add the white wine and reduce almost all of the liquid. Strain the prepared sauce into the skillet. Add the cutlets and their juice. Heat through.

5. Serve the cutlets on 6 warm plates, covered with the sauce.

KAISERSCHNITZEL

SERVES 6

A creamy sauce with lemon juice and lemon zest gives the veal cutlets a tart, vital flavor. Garnished with capers and parsley, this is a pretty dish and can be served with Spaetzle (see Index) or buttered noodles. The Kaiserschnitzel is enhanced by a medium-dry white wine.

Zest of 3 lemons (make sure not to include any of the white portion of the peel), cut into thin strips
1 teaspoon sugar
2 pounds loin or top round of veal, cut into 12 cutlets
1/2 cup clarified butter for sautéing
1 small onion, finely sliced
1/2 cup dry white wine
2 tablespoons capers and their liquid
1 cup heavy cream
2 tablespoons Brown Veal Stock (see Index)
Juice of 1 lemon
Salt and freshly ground white pepper to taste
1/2 bunch parsley, finely chopped

1. Place the lemon zest in a saucepan. Cover with water and the sugar. Boil until the zest has a slightly sweet taste. Remove the zest from the water and allow to cool.

2. Pound the veal and make 2 incisions in the edge of each cutlet to prevent shrinkage.

3. Heat 1/4 cup clarified butter in a skillet and sauté the veal cutlets over medium-high heat until brown outside and pink inside, about 1 1/2 minutes for each side. Remove and keep warm on a covered plate.

4. Degrease the pan by wiping out with a paper towel. Heat 1/4 cup clarified butter and sauté the onion over medium-high heat until golden. Add the white wine and reduce by half. Strain the capers and set aside. Add the caper liquid and reduce 2 to 3 minutes. Reduce the heat to medium, add the cream, and reduce by half, about 8 to 10 minutes.

5. Strain the sauce into a second skillet. Add the veal stock and allow to reduce 1 minute over medium heat. Stir in the lemon juice and lemon zest, and season with salt and pepper to taste.

6. Arrange the cutlets on 6 warm plates and cover with the sauce. Garnish each cutlet with some parsley and capers.

WIENER SCHNITZEL

SERVES 6

Breaded veal cutlets, fried to golden perfection. This simple and rewarding dish was imported into Austria from Milan in the early nineteenth century. It quickly became the national favorite, the ne plus ultra of Viennese cuisine. Garnish the cutlets with bright lemon wedges and serve the traditional way with a leaf or cucumber salad.

6 (6-ounce) cutlets from the top loin of veal
2 eggs
2 tablespoons milk
Flour and bread crumbs for breading
Salt and freshly ground white pepper to taste
1 cup butter
1 cup oil
3 lemons for garnish

1. Pound the veal cutlets with a meat hammer. Make 2 incisions in the edge of each cutlet to prevent shrinkage during the frying.

2. Beat the eggs and milk in one bowl. Place the flour and bread crumbs separately in two more bowls.

3. Salt and pepper the meat. First dip the cutlet in the bowl of flour and shake off the excess. Next dip the cutlet in the egg-milk mixture. Again shake off the excess. Finally dip the cutlet in bread crumbs and shake off the excess. The crumbs should cling only slightly to the cutlet.

4. Heat 1/2 cup of the butter and 1/2 cup of the oil in a skillet

over a high flame until quite hot (325° F.). Fry 3 cutlets about 3 minutes on each side, until golden brown, and then drain on paper towels. Pour out the fat and wipe out the pan with paper towels. Add the remaining butter and oil. Heat over a high flame until hot. Sauté the remaining cutlets as you did the first. Drain them on paper towels.

5. Serve garnished with lemon wedges.

SLICED VEAL STEAKS IN MOREL SAUCE
WITH POTATO DUMPLINGS

SERVES 6

Two sauces distinguish this dish. An aromatic basil-cream enhances the potato dumplings, and a heady reduction of forest mushrooms, Madeira, and stock accompanies the veal. Serve with an attractive array of seasonal vegetables. We find that a full-bodied white wine is a good accompaniment. Try a Gewürztraminer.

1 pound potatoes
1 cup flour (about)
1 egg yolk
Salt and freshly ground white pepper to taste
3 tablespoons sherry vinegar
1/2 cup heavy cream
1 bunch basil, finely chopped
1/3 cup plus 2 tablespoons clarified butter for sautéing
11/2 pounds loin of veal, sliced into 6 steaks
6 shallots, peeled and finely diced
1 cup fresh morels, sliced into fine strips, or 1/2 cup dried
    morels, soaked in Madeira at least 30 minutes, and
    then sliced into fine strips
1/4 cup Madeira
1 cup Brown Veal Stock (see Index)
2 tablespoons butter

1. Boil the potatoes until tender and then peel them. Allow the potatoes to cool. Rice in a meat grinder and set aside.

2. Mix the riced potatoes, 1/2 cup of the flour, and the egg yolk to form the dough. Knead the dough on a tabletop, adding flour as necessary, up to 1 cup, until the dough no longer sticks to the surface. Salt and pepper to taste.

3. Form the dough into 30 small round dumplings. Drop the dumplings into boiling salted water, return to boiling, and cook for 4 to 5 minutes. Remove and refresh in ice water.

4. Pour the sherry vinegar into a saucepan, add the cream, and bring to a boil over medium-high heat. Reduce to a sauce consistency. Add the potato dumplings, chopped basil, and salt and pepper to taste. Keep warm over a low flame.

5. Heat 1/3 cup clarified butter in a skillet and sauté the veal steaks over high heat until they are brown outside and pink inside, about 7 to 10 minutes. Remove and keep warm on a covered plate.

6. Degrease the skillet by wiping it out with a paper towel and add 2 tablespoons clarified butter. Sauté the shallots over medium heat until golden. Add the morels and sauté 3 to 4 minutes. Add the Madeira and reduce almost all of the liquid. Add the veal stock, bring to a boil, and cook 3 to 4 minutes, until reduced by half. Swirl in the 2 tablespoons butter. Salt and pepper to taste.

7. Carve the veal steaks in half lengthwise. Leave one side whole and carve the other into 4 slices still attached at the bottom, forming a fan shape. Place the dumplings and their sauce on the plate near the veal. Pour some meat sauce on the other side of the plate.

MEDALLIONS OF VEAL
WITH CHIVES AND CREAM SAUCE

SERVES 6

A classic demanded again and again by our guests. Lots of gently sautéed chives and a light cream sauce with smoked ham and mushrooms complement the choice veal. Serve with seasonal vegetables and Truffle Crepes (see Index).

2/3 cup clarified butter for sautéing
1/4 pound smoked ham, finely diced (about 1/2 cup diced)
6 medium shallots, finely diced
3/4 cup finely diced white mushroom caps
1/3 cup dry white wine, plus 2 tablespoons for degreasing
1 bay leaf
1/2 cup heavy cream
Juice of 1 lemon
1/3 cup Brown Veal Stock (see Index)
2 1/2 pounds boned saddle of veal, cut into 18 medallions
4 tablespoons butter
2 bunches of chives, chopped
Salt and freshly ground white pepper to taste

1. Heat 1/3 cup clarified butter and sauté the smoked ham. Add the shallots and mushrooms and continue to sauté until they are golden.

2. Add the 1/3 cup white wine and the bay leaf. Reduce almost all of the liquid. Add the cream and bring to a boil. Immediately strain the sauce, reserving the ham, onions, and mushrooms. Discard the bay leaf.

3. Reduce the cream to a sauce consistency. Add the lemon juice and the veal stock, and again reduce to a sauce consistency. Add the ham, mushrooms, and shallots. Set aside.

4. Sauté the veal medallions in 1/3 cup clarified butter over medium-high heat until they are brown outside and pink inside, about 3 to 4 minutes on each side.

5. While the medallions are cooking, heat the 4 tablespoons of butter in a pan, add the chives, and sauté gently 1 minute, being careful that the butter does not burn. Keep warm.

6. When the medallions are done, set aside on a covered plate. Degrease the pan with the remaining 2 tablespoons white wine. Add the prepared sauce and any meat juices that have run onto the covered plate. Season with salt and pepper to taste.

7. Place 3 medallions on the center of each warm plate. Top one with sautéed chives and one with sauce, and leave one plain.

MEDALLIONS OF VEAL WITH
ASPARAGUS SABAYON IN RIESLING SAUCE

SERVES 6

Delectable sautéed medallions of veal are covered with a smooth asparagus sabayon (which can be made in advance of your dinner). The whole is sauced by a Riesling cream with an opulent touch of goose liver. A significant spring dish that recalls the fine dining of the Belle Époque. Serve with an attractive julienne of seasonal vegetables, Château Potatoes (see Index), and a dry Austrian Riesling.

About 1/2 cup clarified butter for sautéing
21/2 pounds tenderloin or top round of veal, cut into 18
    medallions
4 shallots, peeled and finely diced
1/2 cup Riesling
1 cup heavy cream
1/2 cup Brown Veal Stock (see Index)
2 tablespoons Madeira
4 tablespoons fresh or canned goose liver
Salt and freshly ground white pepper to taste

ASPARAGUS SABAYON
1/2 pound asparagus, trimmed
1/4 cup clarified butter for sautéing
2 shallots, peeled and finely diced
Juice of 1 lemon
4 egg yolks
1/3 cup heavy cream
Salt and freshly ground white pepper to taste

1. Cook the asparagus in double their volume of water until tender. Drain the asparagus and cut into 1/2-inch pieces.
2. Heat 1/4 cup clarified butter in a pan and sauté the 2 shallots over medium heat until golden. Add the asparagus and sauté for 5 minutes.

3. Place the asparagus, shallots, lemon juice, and egg yolks in a food processor and puree thoroughly. Transfer to a bowl and whisk the asparagus mixture with the 1/3 cup heavy cream. Season with salt and pepper to taste. The sabayon may be prepared in advance of your dinner and refrigerated.

4. Heat 1/3 cup clarified butter in a skillet and sauté the medallions over medium-high heat until they are brown outside and pink inside, about 3 minutes on each side. Keep warm on a covered plate.

5. Preheat the broiler.

6. Degrease the skillet by wiping it out with a paper towel. Heat 2 tablespoons clarified butter and sauté the 4 shallots until golden. Add the Riesling and reduce by half. Add the 1 cup cream and reduce by half. Add the veal stock and Madeira and again reduce by half.

7. Whisk in the goose liver and immediately remove the sauce from the heat. Season with salt and pepper to taste.

8. Cover 12 of the medallions with the asparagus sabayon and brown under the preheated broiler.

9. Strain the sauce onto 6 warm plates. For each portion, serve 2 medallions with sabayon and a plain medallion on top of the sauce.

VEAL STEAKS WITH CHANTERELLES
IN A BASIL-MINT SAUCE

SERVES 6

A memorable summer celebration! Veal steaks are couched on a rich
bed of sautéed forest mushrooms and highlighted by a fragrant, refreshing herb sauce. Seasonal vegetables and Simple Potato Croquettes (see Index) are suitable side dishes. For a wine we recommend
a Grüner Veltliner Spätlese.

About 2/3 cup clarified butter for sautéing
2¹/2 pounds boned saddle of veal, cut into 6 steaks
1¹/2 cups fresh chanterelles, rinsed, dried on paper towels,
    and torn in half by hand
5 shallots, peeled and finely chopped
Dash of ground thyme
1 clove garlic, peeled
1/2 bunch parsley, finely chopped
Juice of 1 lemon
Salt and freshly ground white pepper to taste
1 bunch fresh basil, rinsed, dried, and finely chopped
1 tablespoon fresh peppermint, rinsed, dried, and finely
    chopped
Dash of sherry vinegar
1/3 cup dry white wine
1 cup heavy cream
1/2 cup Brown Veal Stock (see Index)
4 tablespoons butter

1. Heat 1/3 cup clarified butter in a skillet and sauté the veal
steaks over medium-high heat until brown outside and pink inside,
about 3 to 4 minutes on each side. Remove and keep warm on a
covered plate.

2. Degrease the pan by wiping it out with a paper towel. Heat
1/4 cup clarified butter and sauté the chanterelles. Add half of the
chopped shallots and a dash of thyme. Sauté until golden brown.
Spear the garlic on a kitchen fork and stir through the mixture for 2

to 3 minutes. Add the parsley, lemon juice, and salt and pepper to taste. Allow to reduce for 2 minutes. Remove the mushrooms and any remaining sauce and keep warm on a covered plate.

3. Degrease the pan again and heat 1 tablespoon clarified butter. Sauté the remaining shallots until golden. Add the basil and mint. Sauté 2 to 3 minutes. Add a dash of sherry vinegar and the white wine. Reduce almost all of the liquid. Add the cream and reduce to a sauce consistency. Add the veal stock and again reduce to a sauce consistency. Swirl in the butter and season with salt and pepper to taste. Set aside and keep warm to allow the flavors to meld.

4. Arrange chanterelles in the center of each warm plate. Place a veal steak over the chanterelles and strain sauce all around the mushrooms.

VEAL WITH GLAZED SCALLIONS

SERVES 6

Serve this light summer dish with a bouquet of seasonal vegetables. The baby onions add a zesty touch to the veal.

6 scallions (both green and white parts), thinly sliced
1/3 cup plus 2 tablespoons clarified butter for sautéing
1/4 cup dry white wine
1/2 cup heavy cream
12 tablespoons butter
Salt and freshly ground white pepper to taste
6 (6-ounce) fillets of veal
7 scallions (green portion only), thinly sliced
1 tablespoon sugar

1. Blanch the white portion of the 6 scallions in boiling salted water for 3 to 5 minutes. Refresh in ice water, drain, and set aside.

2. Preheat the oven to 400° F.

3. Begin by preparing the sauce: heat 2 tablespoons clarified butter in a skillet and sauté the green portion of the 6 scallions over medium-high heat for 3 to 4 minutes. Add the white wine and allow to boil for 5 minutes. Puree in a food processor, strain, and return to the skillet. Add the heavy cream and reduce by half. Swirl in 10 tablespoons of the butter. Season with salt and pepper to taste. Set aside and keep warm.

4. Heat 1/3 cup clarified butter in another, ovenproof skillet and quickly sauté the veal fillets over medium-high heat on both sides until golden. Place the skillet in the preheated oven for about 6 minutes. The fillets should be browned outside and pink inside. Remove the fillets and keep warm on a covered plate.

5. To the same skillet add the remaining 2 tablespoons butter and allow to brown slightly. Sauté the blanched and all the remaining green scallions. Add the sugar and heat through a moment, until the scallions are glazed.

6. Carve the veal diagonally, from the top corner on one side to the bottom corner on the opposite side. You will have roughly 2

triangles for each fillet. Pour the scallion sauce in the center of 6 warm plates. Arrange the veal slices in a circular pattern over the sauce. Place the glazed scallions in the middle of each serving.

SLICED CALF'S LIVER IN WALNUT SAUCE

SERVES 6

Ground walnuts provide dramatic texture and flavor, while hazelnut liqueur and sherry vinegar add a fine sweet-piquant note to this uncomplicated liver dish. Serve with colorful glazed carrots or spinach. A rosé or light red wine is recommended.

2/3 cup oil for frying
2 1/2 pounds calf's liver, with skin and sinews removed, and carved into 12 slices
3 tablespoons flour
2 tablespoons butter
4 shallots, peeled and sliced
1/4 cup ground walnuts
2 tablespoons sherry vinegar
3 tablespoons Frangelico liqueur
1 cup Brown Veal Stock (see Index)
Salt and freshly ground white pepper to taste
12 walnut halves for garnish

1. Heat 1/3 cup of the oil in a skillet. Dip both sides of the liver slices in the flour and shake off the excess. Fry half the liver slices over medium-high heat for 2 minutes on each side, until brown outside and still pink inside. Remove and keep warm on a covered plate. Heat the remaining 1/3 cup oil and repeat with the remaining liver slices.

2. Degrease the skillet by wiping it out with a paper towel. Melt 2 tablespoons of butter and sauté the shallots over medium heat until golden. Add the ground walnuts and allow to brown. Add the sherry vinegar and Frangelico, and reduce by half. Add the stock

and reduce all of the liquid to 1/2 cup. Season with salt and pepper to taste.

3. Cut each fried liver slice diagonally in the middle and arrange 4 half slices in a star shape on each warm plate. Strain the sauce over the liver and garnish with the walnut halves.

SAUTÉED SWEETBREAD AND CHICKEN MOUSSE DUMPLINGS IN VERMOUTH SAUCE

SERVES 6

An interesting array of mushrooms accompanies our delicate sweetbreads. Serve with seasonal vegetables and Truffle Crepes (see Index).

2 pounds sweetbreads, cleaned
1 medium carrot, diced
1 celery stalk, diced
1 medium onion, diced
1 leek (white portion only), well rinsed and diced
10 black peppercorns
1 bay leaf
Dash of white vinegar
2 boneless and skinless whole chicken breasts
2 egg whites
1 1/2 cups heavy cream
Juice of 1 lemon
2 tablespoons Madeira
Salt and freshly ground white pepper to taste
About 1 cup clarified butter for sautéing
1 cup fresh chanterelles, rinsed, dried on paper towels, and
    torn in half by hand
1 cup fresh shiitake mushrooms, sliced
1 cup regular mushrooms, sliced
4 shallots, peeled and finely chopped
Pinch of fresh thyme
1/2 cup dry vermouth

1. Blanch the sweetbreads in 1 quart boiling water with the diced vegetables, peppercorns, bay leaf, and vinegar. The sweetbreads should be white outside and pink inside. Refresh the sweetbreads in ice water and then cut them in 24 slices, 4 per person. Set aside. Reserve all of the sweetbread stock resulting from the blanching. Separate 1/4 cup of the stock and reserve it for the sauce.

2. Cut the chicken breasts into 1-inch strips and place with the egg whites, 1/2 cup of the cream, half the lemon juice, the Madeira, and salt and pepper in a food processor. Puree until smooth. Press the mousse through a fine sieve. Place 1 tablespoon of the mousse in the palm of your hand. Smooth it into an oval. Scoop up the mousse with another tablespoon and gently place on a plate. Repeat to form 18 quenelles. Bring the sweetbread stock (less the 1/4 cup) to a slow boil and poach the quenelles for 5 minutes, until tender. Refresh the quenelles in ice water, remove, and set aside.

3. Heat 3/4 cup clarified butter in a pan and sauté all of the mushrooms, the shallots, and a pinch of thyme over medium heat for 10 minutes. Add the vermouth and reduce almost all of the liquid. Add the 1/4 cup of reserved sweetbread stock and allow to reduce for 4 to 5 minutes. Add the remaining 1 cup cream and reduce to a sauce consistency. Stir in the remaining lemon juice. Season with salt and pepper to taste.

4. Heat 1/3 cup clarified butter in a skillet and briefly reheat the sweetbreads. Add the quenelles and sauté 2 to 3 minutes.

5. Pour the sauce onto warm plates and serve 3 dumplings and 4 slices of sweetbreads over the sauce.

CHAPTER 6

Chicken

Chicken has many virtues. It is flavorful, inexpensive, always available, low in calories, easy to prepare, and appropriate at any time of the year. Our recipes demonstrate that, far from being pedestrian, chicken can be the basis for exciting combinations with fruit, herbs, and seasonings. We know you'll enjoy our elegant fried chicken with tarragon sauce, serene chicken with tart apple slices, savory paprika chicken, mellow émincé of chicken in Riesling, and zesty chicken with ginger. Each has its own distinctive appeal and may be handsomely presented with the simplest side dishes. The following recipes are fun to prepare and perfect for company or informal family dinners.

Here are several good wines to complement most chicken dishes: Grüner Veltliner, Pinot Blanc, Riesling, Pinot Chardonnay, or Gumpoldskirchner.

CHICKEN BREAST IN TARRAGON SAUCE

SERVES 6

Since the early eighteenth century, Backhendl, golden fried chicken garnished with lemon wedges, has been a staple of Viennese cuisine. Unlike Southern fried chicken, the Viennese version is dipped first in flour, then in egg, and lastly in bread crumbs. Here you'll find an elegant variation of the Austrian favorite. Boneless chicken breasts are first smoothed with a mushroom velouté, then breaded and fried the traditional way. A zesty tarragon sauce gives the fried chicken a contemporary accent. Our hint: fresh tarragon is essential. Garnish our Backhendl with glazed carrots, broccoli, or Truffle Crepes (see Index).

About 3/4 cup clarified butter for sautéing
12 white mushrooms, sliced
Juice of 1 lemon
4 tablespoons butter
1/4 cup flour, plus flour to coat the chicken
1/2 cup Chicken Stock (see Index)
Salt and freshly ground white pepper to taste
6 (8-ounce) boneless and skinless chicken breast halves
2 eggs
Bread crumbs for breading
4 shallots, peeled and finely chopped
1 bunch tarragon, chopped
2 tablespoons tarragon vinegar
1 cup heavy cream
1/3 cup Brown Veal Stock (see Index)
1 bunch parsley, finely chopped

1. To prepare the velouté, first heat 1/3 cup clarified butter in a skillet and briefly sauté the mushrooms over medium heat for 3 to 4 minutes. Add the lemon juice and remove the pan from the heat. Set aside.

2. Melt the 4 tablespoons of butter in a pot. Stir in the flour and then add the chicken stock. Allow the stock to boil for 5 minutes. Add the mushrooms and lemon juice. Allow to boil another

minute. If the velouté becomes too thick (like heavy cream) stir in a little water. Season with salt and pepper to taste.

3. While the velouté is still quite hot, spoon it over the chicken breasts. Set aside and allow to cool.

4. Place some flour, the eggs, and some bread crumbs in separate bowls. Dip the chicken breasts in flour and shake off the excess. Then dip them in the egg and again shake off the excess. Finally dip the breasts in bread crumbs and shake off the excess.

5. Heat 1/3 cup clarified butter in a skillet and sauté 3 of the chicken breasts over medium-high heat until they are golden brown, about 3 to 4 minutes on each side. Remove the breasts and keep warm on a covered dish. Repeat with the remaining breasts.

6. Heat 2 tablespoons clarified butter in a saucepan and sauté the shallots over medium heat until golden. Add the tarragon and tarragon vinegar and allow to reduce 4 to 5 minutes. Add the cream and reduce to a sauce consistency. Add the brown stock and again reduce to a sauce consistency. Stir in the parsley and season with salt and pepper to taste.

7. Pour the sauce onto 6 warm plates and serve the chicken over the sauce.

CHICKEN BREAST PRINZ EUGEN
Chicken with Apples in Calvados Cream Sauce

SERVES 6

This dish was named for the Austrian hero of the late seventeenth and early eighteenth centuries Prince Eugene, who was responsible for the building of one of the most beautiful palaces in Vienna, the Belvedere.

Tender slices of white meat alternate with tangy slices of sautéed apple mellowed with a seductive apple-brandy cream sauce. This easy combination of poultry, fruit, and Calvados evokes the bountiful orchards of Normandy. Try it with white rice and a leaf salad. A pleasing wine to accompany this meal is the light, dry Pinot Blanc by Klosterkeller Siegendorf.

About 3/4 cup clarified butter for sautéing
6 (8-ounce) chicken breast halves, deboned and skinned
2 Granny Smith apples, peeled, cored, and sliced in 2-inch-thick sections (cut the peel into slivers and reserve it for making the sauce)
4 shallots, finely chopped
1/3 cup Calvados
1/4 cup Chicken Stock (see Index)
1 cup heavy cream
Salt and freshly ground white pepper to taste
2 tablespoons butter

1. Preheat the oven to 500° F.

2. Heat 1/3 cup clarified butter in an overproof skillet and sauté 3 of the chicken breasts over medium-high heat, first on the meat side and then on the skin side, about 3 to 4 minutes on each side. Transfer the chicken to the oven and bake for 10 minutes. Heat another 1/3 cup clarified butter and repeat with the remaining 3 breasts. Remove and keep warm on a covered plate.

2. Heat 3 tablespoons clarified butter in the same pan and sauté the apple slices over medium heat. Remove and keep warm on a covered plate.

3. Next sauté the shallots and apple peel until the shallots are

golden. Add the Calvados and chicken stock. Reduce by half. Add the cream and reduce to a sauce consistency. Strain the sauce into another pan. Season with salt and pepper to taste. Swirl in the 2 tablespoons butter.

4. Cut each chicken breast into 5 slices. Place an apple slice between each 2 slices of chicken and cover with the Calvados sauce.

PAPRIKAHUHN
Paprika Chicken

SERVES 6

Colorful and savory, this chicken goulash needs nothing more than Spaetzle (see Index) to make a simple yet delicious meal. Paprika is a mainstay of Austro-Hungarian cooking. We suggest using sweet Hungarian paprika for authenticity.

2/3 **cup vegetable oil for sautéing**
3 **whole smallish chickens, cut in half, backbones removed**
Salt and freshly ground white pepper to taste
4 **medium onions, sliced**
2 **sweet red peppers, with seeds removed, diced**
1 **tablespoon tomato paste**
2 **tablespoons sweet Hungarian paprika**
2½ **cups Chicken Stock or more (see Index)**
1 **cup heavy cream**

1. Preheat the oven to 300° F.

2. Heat ⅓ cup oil in a skillet. Season the chicken with salt and pepper. Sauté on the meat side over medium-high heat for 7 to 8 minutes, until golden; turn, and sauté on the other side for 7 to 8 minutes, until golden. Remove the chicken from the pan.

3. Degrease the pan by wiping it out with a paper towel. Sauté the onions in ⅓ cup oil over medium heat until golden. Add the red peppers and sauté 4 to 5 minutes. Stir in the tomato paste. Add the paprika and immediately pour in 1½ cups of the chicken stock. Reduce by half. Add the cup of heavy cream and reduce to a sauce consistency.

4. Arrange the chicken in a baking pan. Pour 1 cup of chicken stock over it, add the sauce, cover, and bake 30 minutes. Check occasionally to make sure that the sauce is not becoming too thick. Add a little chicken broth or water if necessary.

5. Remove the chicken and set aside on a covered plate. Strain the sauce and blend it to a smooth consistency.

6. Carve the chicken and serve with the paprika sauce and a generous helping of Spaetzle.

ÉMINCÉ OF CHICKEN WITH RIESLING SAUCE

SERVES 6

Riesling gives brilliant, fruity flavor to this classic one-dish cassoulet of chicken and vegetables. Serve with Spaetzle (see Index) and accompany with the same wine used for cooking.

1 carrot, peeled and cut à la julienne, into thin strips
1/2 celery root (celeriac), cut à la julienne
1/2 yellow turnip, peeled and cut à la julienne
1 parsley root, cut à la julienne
6 (8-ounce) chicken breast halves, deboned and skin
    removed
Salt and freshly ground white pepper to taste
2/3 cup clarified butter
1 large onion, thinly sliced
10 white mushroom heads, sliced
1 cup Riesling
1 cup heavy cream
1/4 cup Chicken Stock (see Index)
1 tablespoon butter

1. Separately blanch the julienned vegetables in boiling water, then refresh in ice water. Combine once they are cooled.

2. Cut the chicken breasts against the grain into 1/4-inch-thick slices. Season with salt and pepper to taste.

3. Heat 1/3 cup clarified butter in a skillet and sauté the chicken over medium-high heat on each side until golden. Remove and set aside on a covered plate.

4. Add 1/3 cup clarified butter to the skillet and sauté the onion and mushrooms. Add the Riesling and vegetables. Reduce all of the liquid. Remove the vegetable mixture and set aside.

5. Add the cream and chicken stock to the skillet. Reduce to a sauce consistency. Blend the sauce, and add the chicken and vegetables. Season with salt and pepper to taste. Reheat a moment, then swirl in the butter.

CHICKEN CUTLETS ENHANCED WITH
GINGER AND SCALLIONS

SERVES 6

Ginger adds a snappy, exuberant accent to chicken. We find that the classic oriental pairing of ginger and scallions marries beautifully with the delicate cream sauce used in occidental cuisine. Serve with boiled new potatoes. Our wine recommendation: Riesling Spätlese Ried-Klaus by Josef Jamek.

1 cup Rose's unsweetened lime juice
Juice of 1 fresh lime
1 medium ginger root
6 (8-ounce) chicken breast halves
12 scallions
1/2 medium carrot, peeled and cut into thin round slices
2 medium stalks celery, strings removed, and finely sliced
1 leek (white portion only), well rinsed and finely sliced
Salt and freshly ground white pepper to taste
1/3 cup plus 1/4 cup clarified butter
6 scallions (white portion only), finely sliced
2 cups Chicken Stock (see Index)
1/4 cup heavy cream
4 tablespoons butter

1. Mix the Rose's lime juice and the juice of the fresh lime in a bowl. Peel the ginger root and julienne. Marinate in the lime juice for 1 hour.

2. Bone the chicken breasts, cover with plastic wrap, and pound very thin.

3. Cut off the white portion of the 12 scallions and set aside for garnishing. Chop the green portion.

4. Place the chicken in an ample pan. Pour the lime juice and ginger over it. Add the chopped green scallions, carrot, celery, and leek. Cover and marinate in the refrigerator for 12 hours or overnight.

5. Remove the chicken; sprinkle with salt and pepper. Heat 1/3

cup clarified butter in a skillet and sauté the chicken over medium heat, for about 3 to 4 minutes on each side. Set aside on a covered plate.

6. Heat 1/4 cup clarified butter and sauté the white portion of the 6 scallions over medium heat for 4 to 5 minutes. Strain the vegetables from the marinade and sauté for 4 to 5 minutes.

7. Add the remaining marinade to the vegetables and scallions. Reduce almost all of the liquid. Add the chicken stock and reduce by half. Add the cream and reduce to a sauce consistency. Swirl in the butter to bind the sauce.

8. Arrange the chicken on 6 plates, pour the sauce over it, and garnish with the reserved scallions.

CHAPTER 7

From the Hunt Table

Since the Middle Ages, game dishes have been an essential part of Austrian cuisine. Originally only the land-owning aristocracy, who retained the sole privilege of hunting, could enjoy this fare. During the nineteenth century, however, hunting became open to everyone, and recipes for game dishes could be found in the cookbooks of the middle class. In the 1880s the Wildbretmarkt, the game market in Vienna, became famous across the empire for its variety of rabbit, quail, duck, venison, and other game delicacies.

Today hunting remains a popular sport in Austria. Here we've included some traditional recipes as well as our innovative and imaginative preparations—all artfully designed to enhance the rich and sublime flavors of game.

The best wines to accompany game are Jochinger St.-Laurent, Cabernet-Merlot, Austrian Pinot Noir, Blau-Fränkisch, Corton, Vosne-Romanée, Beaune, Clos des Mouches, Cabernet Sauvignon.

DUCK BREAST AND BLUEBERRY SAUCE

SERVES 6

Succulent slices of duck in a pool of sweet-tart blueberry sauce. Serve with wild rice, Potato Croquettes Rolled in Almonds (see Index), or seasonal vegetables. Our wine recommendation: Pinot Noir Spätlese by Klosterkeller Siegendorf.

6 boned duck breast halves
Salt and freshly ground white pepper to taste
1/3 cup oil for sautéing
1 teaspoon sugar
1 teaspoon sherry vinegar
2 teaspoons cassis
1 cup Brown Veal Stock (see Index)
2 cups heavy cream
**3/4 cup blueberries, rinsed, drained, and patted dry on
    paper towels**
2 tablespoons butter

1. Preheat the oven to 400° F.
2. Make a cross-shaped incision on the skin side of each duck breast and sprinkle with salt and pepper.
3. Heat 1/3 cup oil in an ovenproof skillet and sauté the duck breasts over medium-high heat, first on the skin side and then on the side without skin, about 4 to 5 minutes on each side. Place the skillet in the preheated oven for 4 to 5 minutes, until the breasts are browned outside and pink inside. Keep the duck warm, skin side down, on a covered plate.
4. Pour off the grease from the skillet. Add the sugar, sherry vinegar, and then the cassis. Reduce by half. Add the stock and reduce to a third of the original amount. Add the cream and blueberries and reduce to a sauce consistency. Swirl in the butter and season with salt and pepper to taste. Strain the sauce and keep it warm over a low flame.
5. Pour the blueberry sauce onto 6 warm plates. Cut the duck breast against the grain into thin slices and arrange in fan shapes over the sauce.

DUCK BREAST AND PLUM SAUCE

SERVES 6

Lightly sautéed duck and the sweetness of a brandied plum sauce—a classic! Perfect served with wild rice or Scallion Potatoes (see Index).

**6 duck breasts, boned and halved (reserve the bones to
     prepare a stock)**
Salt and freshly ground white pepper to taste
8 plums, with pits removed
1/3 cup oil for sautéing
2 tablespoons sugar
2 tablespoons sherry vinegar
4 tablespoons plum brandy
3/4 cup duck stock*
2 tablespoons butter

1. Preheat the oven to 400° F.
2. Make a cross-shaped incision on the skin side of each duck breast. Sprinkle with salt and pepper.
3. Cut 2 plums into small cubes and cut the remaining 6 in halves for garnishing.
4. Heat 1/3 cup oil in an ovenproof skillet and sauté the duck breasts over medium-high heat, first on the side without the skin and then on the skin side, for 4 to 5 minutes on each side. Place the skillet in the preheated oven for 4 to 5 minutes, until the duck is browned outside and pink inside. Keep the duck breasts warm on a covered plate, skin side down to prevent further cooking.
5. In the skillet, sauté the plum cubes and sugar over medium heat. Add the sherry vinegar and reduce by half. Add the plum brandy and reduce by half. Add the duck stock and reduce to a sauce consistency. Swirl in the butter, season with salt and pepper, and strain the sauce. Pour the sauce into a pan.
6. Add the 12 plum halves to the saucepan and poach over

---

* For duck stock, follow the directions in Chicken Stock (see Index), substituting duck bones for chicken bones.

medium heat for a minute. Remove the plums from the sauce and keep warm on a covered plate.

7. Pour the plum sauce onto 6 warm plates. Cut the duck breast against the grain into thin slices (aiguilettes). Arrange the duck in fan shapes on the sauce and garnish each portion with 2 plum halves, also cut in fan shapes.

CORNISH HENS STUFFED WITH CHICKEN MOUSSE AND CHANTERELLES

SERVES 6

The woodsy bouquet of forest mushrooms gives this dish European flair. Memorable served on a crisp autumn evening with Champagne Cabbage (see Index), wild rice, seasonal vegetables, or Duchesse Potatoes (see Index). A full-bodied red wine enhances the Cornish game hens.

1/3 cup heavy cream
1 (8-ounce) boneless chicken breast half, with fat removed
1 egg yolk
About 1 cup oil for sautéing
1/4 cup fresh chanterelles, rinsed, dried on paper towels,
    and torn in half by hand
2 shallots, peeled and finely diced
Pinch of thyme
Salt and freshly ground white pepper to taste
6 (1-pound) Cornish game hens, boned, leaving breast and
    leg whole (your butcher can do this for you), with
    bones reserved for preparing stock
4 shallots, cut in slices
1 tablespoon tarragon vinegar
1 cup Chicken Stock (see Index) made with the reserved
    Cornish hen bones, or canned consommé
8 tablespoons butter
1 bunch fresh tarragon, rinsed, dried, and finely chopped

1. Place the heavy cream and boneless chicken breast in a food processor and puree to a smooth consistency. Press through a fine sieve, then stir in the egg yolk and set aside.

2. Heat 2 tablespoons oil in a skillet and sauté the chanterelles over medium heat for 4 minutes. Add the 2 finely diced shallots, and brown. Season with a dash of thyme and salt and white pepper to taste. Set aside to cool.

3. When the chanterelles and shallots are cool, mix with the chicken mousse.

4. Preheat the oven to 375° F.

5. Cut off the bony leg tips of the game hens. Stuff the birds with the mousse and sew them shut so the filling doesn't ooze out.

6. Heat 1/3 cup oil in a skillet and sauté 3 of the birds over medium-high heat for 3 to 4 minutes on each side, until brown. Heat another 1/3 cup oil and repeat with the remaining hens. Place all the birds in a roasting pan and roast in the oven for 15 minutes. When done, remove and keep warm on a covered plate.

7. Meantime, heat 2 tablespoons oil in a skillet and sauté the 4 sliced shallots until transparent. Add the tarragon vinegar and reduce almost all of the liquid.

8. Add the cup of stock, bring to a boil, and reduce by half.

9. Swirl in the butter. Stir in the fresh tarragon, and set aside.

10. Cut each hen in half lengthwise. Pour some sauce on each plate. Place one half hen mousse side up and the other mousse side down over the sauce.

QUAILS WITH WALNUT STUFFING
IN FRANGELICO SAUCE

SERVES 6

The renowned epicure Brillat-Savarin once said of these game birds: "A plump little quail pleases equally for its taste, its form, and its color." We find this quail stuffed with a mixture of nuts particularly pleasing. A fitting wine is the light Pinot Noir Spätlese by Klosterkeller Siegendorf.

About 1 cup oil for sautéing
4 tablespoons ground walnuts
2 tablespoons ground hazelnuts
2 tablespoons whole pine nuts
1 pound white bread, crust removed and cut into 1/2-inch
        cubes
1/4 cup heavy cream
2 egg yolks
1 whole egg
Salt and freshly ground white pepper to taste
12 quails, boned from the backbone, leaving the breasts
        whole (your butcher can do this), with bones reserved
        for preparing stock
6 shallots, peeled and thinly sliced
2 tablespoons Frangelico liqueur
1 teaspoon sugar
1 teaspoon sherry vinegar
1 cup Quail Stock (see Index) or strong Chicken Stock (see
        Index)
1 tablespoon butter

1. Heat 2 tablespoons of oil and sauté all of the nuts over medium heat for 2 to 3 minutes. Set aside and allow to cool.

2. Soak the bread cubes in the heavy cream until soft. Add the egg yolks and whole egg. Stir the mixture and then mash the bread cubes.

3. Add the bread mixture to the cooled nuts. Season with salt and pepper to taste.

4. Preheat the oven to 400° F.

5. Stuff the quails with the bread and nut mixture. Wrap a piece of aluminum foil over the back of each quail and around both ends to seal in the mousse.

6. Heat 1/3 oil in a skillet and sauté 6 quails breast side down over medium-high heat until browned, about 4 to 5 minutes. Add another 1/3 cup oil and repeat with the remaining quails. Place all the birds, aluminum side down, in a roasting pan and roast in the preheated oven for 5 to 7 minutes. Remove from the oven and keep the quail warm on a covered plate.

7. In a skillet, heat 2 tablespoons oil and sauté the shallots over medium heat until transparent, about 5 minutes. Add the Frangelico and the sugar. Bring to a boil for a moment.

8. Add the sherry vinegar and reduce almost all of the liquid. Add the stock, bring to a boil, and reduce to a sauce consistency.

9. Swirl in the butter. Season with salt and pepper to taste. Strain the sauce through a sieve.

10. Remove the foil from the quails. Pour some sauce on each plate. Serve 6 quails whole and 6 cut in half lengthwise. Place a whole quail in the center of each plate with a half on either side.

QUAIL AND SQUAB BREASTS WITH GREEN FIGS

SERVES 6

Figs are a magnificent fruit, evoking the sensual beauty and ripe abundance of the fall season. Their plump sweetness intensifies the flavor of these little game birds. Serve simply with colorful glazed carrots or snow peas. A full-bodied red wine is all that's needed to round out this festive and autumnal meal.

8 fresh green figs, rinsed and peeled
1/2 cup oil for sautéing
6 boned quail breasts, with bones reserved for preparing
　　the stock
6 boned squab breasts, with bones reserved for preparing
　　the stock
1/4 cup port wine
1 tablespoon sugar
1 teaspoon sherry vinegar
1 cup Quail or Squab Stock (see Index) or Brown Veal
　　Stock (see Index)
2 tablespoons butter
Salt and freshly ground white pepper to taste

1. Cut 6 of the peeled figs in half. Scrape off and reserve the seeds for cooking. Leave 2 peeled figs whole.

2. Heat 1/2 cup oil in a skillet and sauté the boned quail and squab breasts over medium-high heat for about 4 to 5 minutes, until brown outside and pink inside. Keep warm on a covered plate, skin side down.

3. In the skillet, briefly sauté the 6 halved figs, about 3 to 4 minutes. Add the port, bring to a boil, and poach over medium heat for 30 seconds.

4. Add the 2 whole figs to the skillet, as well as the fig seeds, sugar, and sherry vinegar. Reduce by half. Add the stock and again reduce by half. Strain the sauce, swirl in the butter, and season with salt and pepper to taste.

5. Carve the squab and quail breasts against the grain into thin slices. Pour the sauce onto 6 warm plates and arrange the meat in fan shapes on the sauce. Garnish each portion with 2 poached fig halves.

The following are recipes for autumn assortments of game with fruit or herbs, scented truffles or wild mushrooms. These fall dishes celebrate the abundance of forest and orchard.

ESCALOPES OF VENISON
WITH LENTILS AND CHANTERELLES

SERVES 6

Robust in character, this venison may be accompanied by Potato
Noodles, Viennese Red Cabbage, Champagne Cabbage, or luxurious
Truffle Crepes (see Index for all).

1 small carrot, peeled
1/2 small white turnip, peeled
1/2 leek (white portion only), well rinsed and trimmed
2/3 cup oil for sautéing
12 (3-ounce) cutlets from leg of venison, pounded and
    sprinkled with salt and pepper
3 shallots, peeled and finely sliced
4 ounces lean bacon, cut into fine cubes (about 1/3 cup
    cubed)
3/4 cup chanterelles, rinsed, dried on paper towels, and torn
    in half by hand
1/2 cup dry red wine
1 cup Brown Game Stock (see Index)
Salt and freshly ground white pepper to taste
4 tablespoons butter
6 tablespoons boiled lentils

1. Blanch the carrot, turnip, and leek separately in boiling water, then refresh in ice water. Mince and set aside.

2. Heat 1/3 cup oil in a skillet and sauté half the venison cutlets
over medium-high heat until browned outside and pink inside,
about 2 to 3 minutes each side. Remove and keep warm on a covered
plate. Add another 1/3 cup oil and repeat with the remaining cutlets.

3. Add the shallots, bacon cubes, and chanterelles to the skillet
and sauté for a moment. Remove and also keep warm on a separate
covered plate.

4. To prepare the sauce, add the red wine to the skillet and
reduce by half over medium heat. Add the stock and again reduce

by half. Stir any juices from the venison on the covered plate into the sauce. Season with salt and pepper to taste, then swirl in the butter. Add the blanched vegetables, the boiled lentils, and the mixture of chanterelles, shallots, and bacon. Bring to a boil and cook 2 to 3 minutes.

5. Place 2 cutlets on each warm plate. Cover one with sauce and leave the other plain.

RABBIT SADDLE FILLETS AND
PHEASANT BREASTS IN MARJORAM SAUCE

SERVES 6

Marjoram blends beautifully with this delicate combination of game (fresh marjoram is essential). Serve with mushroom rice or sautéed forest mushrooms.

About 3/4 cup oil for sautéing
3 boned saddles of rabbit, sprinkled with salt and pepper
3 whole pheasant breasts, boned, sprinkled with salt and
     pepper
1/3 cup chopped onion
1/4 cup chopped fresh marjoram
1 tablespoon sherry vinegar
1 cup Brown Game Stock (see Index)
1/4 cup dry red wine
4 tablespoons butter
Salt and freshly ground white pepper to taste

1. Preheat the oven to 400° F.

2. Heat 1/3 cup oil in an ovenproof skillet and sauté the rabbit fillets over medium-high heat for approximately 3 minutes on each side. The rabbit should remain pink inside. Remove and keep warm on a covered plate.

3. In the same skillet, add another 1/3 cup oil and sauté the pheasant breasts over medium-high heat for 3 to 4 minutes on each side. Place the skillet in the oven for 4 to 5 minutes. Remove the pheasant and keep warm with the rabbit on the covered plate.

4. To prepare the marjoram sauce, heat 2 tablespoons oil in the same skillet and sauté the onion until transparent. Add the marjoram and sherry vinegar. Stir in the stock and the red wine, bring to a boil, and reduce by half. Strain the sauce and then swirl in the butter. Season with salt and pepper to taste. Keep the sauce warm over a low flame.

5. Slice the rabbit and pheasant thinly against the grain. Pour the sauce onto 6 warm plates. Arrange a semicircle of rabbit and a

semicircle of pheasant. In the center place the mushroom rice or sautéed forest mushrooms.

SAUTÉED VENISON FILLETS AND RED CURRANT SAUCE

SERVES 6

An elegant and classic pairing. Serve with Viennese Red Cabbage, Zucchini Tartlet, or Potato Strudel (see Index for all). The best time for fresh currants is around July, but canned currants are available all year round and are a perfectly acceptable substitute.

1/3 cup oil for sautéing
6 whole venison fillets (tenderloin of venison), trimmed of
**   fat and sprinkled with salt and pepper**
3 tablespoons red currants, plus 1 tablespoon for
**   garnishing**
2 tablespoons sugar
1 teaspoon sherry vinegar
3/4 cup Brown Game Stock (see Index)
2 tablespoons butter
Salt and freshly ground white pepper to taste

1. Heat 1/3 cup oil in a skillet and sauté the venison fillets over medium-high heat for about 3 minutes on each side. They should be brown outside and pink inside. Remove and keep warm on a covered plate.

2. Add the 3 tablespoons currants, the sugar, and sherry vinegar to the skillet and sauté 3 to 4 minutes. Add the stock, bring to a boil, and reduce by half. Strain the sauce and then swirl in the butter. Season with salt and pepper to taste. Keep warm over a low flame.

3. Carve the venison fillets against the grain into long slices. Pour the currant sauce onto 6 warm plates and arrange the venison slices in a circular pattern on the sauce. Garnish with currants.

GAME PLATE WITH A BLACK CURRANT SAUCE

SERVES 6

A munificent feast of pheasant, venison, and hare, studded with tart fruit. Suitable accompaniments: Viennese Red Cabbage (see Index), Champagne Cabbage (see Index), Dumplings in a Napkin (see Index), or glazed chestnuts. This noble fare calls for a smooth burgundy.

1 cup plus 2 tablespoons oil for frying
1½ pounds boned saddle of venison, cut into 6 portions and sprinkled with salt and pepper
1½ pounds boned saddle of hare, cut into 6 portions and sprinkled with salt and pepper
3 boned pheasant breasts, sprinkled with salt and pepper
6 shallots, peeled and finely sliced
½ cup black currants for cooking, plus 2 tablespoons for garnishing
2 teaspoons sugar
2 teaspoons sherry vinegar
2 tablespoons cassis
1 cup Brown Game Stock (see Index)
4 tablespoons butter
Salt and freshly ground pepper to taste

1. Preheat the oven to 400° F.

2. Heat ⅓ cup oil in a skillet and sauté the venison over medium-high heat until it is brown outside and pink inside. Remove and keep warm on a covered plate.

3. Add another ⅓ cup oil to the skillet and sauté the hare until it is pink inside and brown outside. Remove and keep warm on a separate covered plate.

4. Heat ⅓ cup oil in a separate ovenproof skillet and sauté the pheasant breasts over medium-high heat for 3 to 4 minutes. Place the skillet in the oven for 4 to 5 minutes. Remove and keep the pheasant warm on another covered plate.

5. In the skillet used to cook the venison and the hare, heat 2 tablespoons oil and sauté the shallots and the ½ cup currants over

medium heat for 3 to 4 minutes. Add the sugar. Then add the vinegar and cassis. Bring to a boil and reduce all of the liquid. Add the stock, bring to a boil, and reduce by half. Strain the sauce and then swirl in the butter. Season with salt and pepper to taste and keep warm over a low flame.

6. Carve the meat against the grain into fine slices. Pour some sauce on each warm plate. Arrange the 3 meats in triangles, forming an attractive star pattern. The side dish should be served on a separate plate.

MEDALLIONS OF VENISON AND BLACK TRUFFLES SERVED WITH A PORT WINE SAUCE

SERVES 6

Aromatic truffles give this venison a luxurious touch. Serve with Viennese Red Cabbage (see Index), Champagne Cabbage (see Index), Potato Croquettes Rolled in Almonds (see Index), or sautéed wild mushrooms. A truly sublime meal, especially with a bottle of smooth red wine.

6 thin slices of fresh black truffle
2 tablespoons cognac
2 tablespoons Madeira
1/2 cup plus 1/3 cup oil for sautéing
2 pounds venison bones, chopped into small cubes with a cleaver (ask your specialty butcher to reserve and prepare the bones)
1 carrot, peeled and finely chopped
2 onions, minced
1 leek (white portion only), well rinsed and coarsely chopped
Stems of 1 bunch of parsley
1 cup Brown Game Stock (see Index)
Salt and freshly ground white pepper to taste
2 1/2 pounds boned saddle of venison, cut into 12 medallions
2 tablespoons butter

1. Marinate the slices of truffle in the cognac and Madeira.

2. Heat 1/2 cup oil in a skillet and brown the chopped venison bones over high heat. Add all of the vegetables and the parsley stems and sauté until browned. Strain the truffles and add the Madeira and cognac to the skillet. Add the cup of game stock, bring to a boil, and reduce by half. Strain the sauce. Season with salt and pepper to taste. Keep warm over a low flame.

3. Next heat 1/3 cup oil in a skillet over medium-high heat and

sauté the medallions of venison until medium-rare, about 2 to 3 minutes on each side. Remove the meat and keep warm on a covered plate.

4. Cool the skillet with some water and empty it. Pour the sauce into the skillet and swirl in the butter.

5. Pour the sauce onto warm plates. Serve 2 medallions per person. One medallion should remain whole; slice the other in the middle and insert a marinated truffle. Place the medallion with the truffle over the other.

CHAPTER 8

Beef, Lamb, and Pork

Meat dishes no longer have to be heavy, filling fare. Even the most calorie-conscious will crave these light beef, lamb, and pork preparations. Serve a light appetizer and then indulge in a hearty Viennese-style sirloin, a juicy pork chop accented with sorrel or capers, or fine lamb medallions smothered with forest mushrooms.

Austrians are known for their remarkable grilled beef preparations. The following are recipes for the most popular Rostbraten: impressive, easy, and particularly delicious ways to treat your guests to a fine cut of sirloin.

ESTERHAZY-ROSTBRATEN
Sirloin of Beef à la Esterhazy

SERVES 6

This traditional favorite was named after a family of wealthy aristocrats whose castles and churches are scattered throughout the Austrian province of Burgenland. The Esterhazys were known as music lovers, particularly as patrons of Haydn, Schubert, and Liszt. Many fine dishes in Austrian cuisine carry the Esterhazy name.

The sirloin à la Esterhazy is accompanied by a hearty sauce with vegetables. It may be served simply with Spaetzle (see Index) or Château Potatoes (see Index).

10 white peppercorns
1 bay leaf
1 medium carrot, peeled and cut à la julienne, into thin
**   strips**
1 yellow turnip, peeled and cut à la julienne (about 2 cups)
1 medium celery root (celeriac), cut à la julienne
1 cup clarified butter for sautéing
6 (7-ounce) slices of sirloin
1 medium white onion, peeled and finely chopped
1/3 cup cognac
1/2 cup heavy cream
1 cup Brown Beef Stock (see Index)
Juice of 1 lemon
1 tablespoon butter
Salt and freshly ground white pepper to taste
Sour cream (optional, for garnishing)

1. Bring 4 cups of water to a boil. Add the peppercorns and bay leaf. Briefly and separately blanch the carrot, turnip, and celery root. Refresh the vegetables in ice water and set aside. Reserve the vegetable stock resulting from the blanching and reduce to 1/3 cup. Remove the bay leaf and peppercorns.

2. Heat 2/3 cup clarified butter in a skillet and sauté the sirloin

over medium-high heat until brown outside and medium-rare inside. Keep warm on a covered plate.

3. Degrease the pan. Heat 1/3 cup clarified butter and sauté the onion over medium heat until golden. Add the cognac and reduce 3 to 5 minutes. Add the vegetable stock and again reduce 4 to 5 minutes over medium-high heat. Add the cream, lower heat to medium, and reduce by half.

4. Add the beef stock and once more reduce by half. Add the lemon juice and any meat juices from the covered plate. Drain the vegetables and stir them into the sauce. Swirl in the butter and season with salt and pepper to taste.

5. Place the meat on plates, topped with the sauce. The sirloin may be garnished with a swirled piping of sour cream, pressed through a pastry bag.

ZWIEBELROSTBRATEN

SERVES 6

Juicy sirloin steak topped with crunchy fried onions. Pickle juice adds a subtle tang to the robust stock-cognac reduction sauce. This quick and easy dish is wonderful with seasonal vegetables and Rosti Potatoes (see Index) on the side. Try a full-bodied red wine. We suggest St.-Laurent, Cabernet, or Austrian Pinot Noir.

4 cups oil for frying the onions
3 white onions, peeled and cut crosswise into thin round
**   slices**
Flour for the onions
2/3 cup clarified butter for sautéing
6 (7-ounce) slices of sirloin
1/3 cup cognac
1/3 cup cornichon pickle juice
1 cup Brown Beef Stock (see Index)
1 tablespoon butter
1 tablespoon Dijon mustard
Salt and freshly ground white pepper to taste

1. Heat the 4 cups of oil in a pot. Meanwhile, dip the onion slices in some flour and pat to remove the excess. When the oil is hot, fry the onions until they are golden. Remove the onions from the oil, drain on paper towels, and keep warm on the stove top.

2. Heat 2/3 cup clarified butter in a skillet and sauté the sirloin slowly over medium-high heat until brown outside and medium-rare inside. Keep the sirloin warm on a covered plate.

3. Degrease the skillet by wiping it out with a paper towel and add the cognac and pickle juice. Reduce almost all of the liquid. Add the beef stock and reduce by half.

4. Lower the heat. Whisk in the butter and mustard at the same time. Be sure to whisk well to avoid having clumps of mustard. Add any meat juices from the sirloin on the covered plate and stir well. Season with salt and pepper to taste.

5. Place the meat on warm plates. Pour the sauce over the meat and sprinkle with fried onions.

VANILLA-ROSTBRATEN
Sirloin Steak with Garlic

SERVES 6

Until the nineteenth century, spices from the East could be afforded only by the wealthy. The populace made use of those seasonings which they could grow in their own gardens. Garlic came to be known in popular parlance as the "poor man's vanilla." Hence the misnomer of this Viennese specialty. Note that blanching the garlic and processing it with butter gives the sirloin sauce a mild but pungent flavor.

4 garlic cloves
1 tablespoon butter
1/3 cup clarified butter for sautéing
6 (7-ounce) slices of sirloin
1/3 cup Madeira
1/3 cup cornichon pickle juice
1 cup Brown Beef Stock (see Index)
1/2 bunch parsley, chopped
Salt and freshly ground white pepper to taste

1. Peel the garlic cloves and blanch briefly in boiling water; then refresh in ice water. Chop the garlic in a food processor with the 1 tablespoon butter.

2. Heat the clarified butter and sauté the sirloin steaks over medium-high heat until brown outside and medium-rare inside. Remove and keep warm on a covered plate.

3. Degrease the pan by wiping it out with a paper towel. Add the Madeira and pickle juice and reduce almost all of the liquid. Add the beef stock and reduce by three quarters.

4. Swirl in the prepared garlic butter with a whisk. Add any meat juices from the covered plate and reduce to a sauce consistency. Add the chopped parsley, and season with salt and pepper to taste.

5. Place the sirloin slices on warm plates and pour the sauce over them.

GIRARDI-ROSTBRATEN
Sirloin Steak à la Girardi

SERVES 6

Alexander Girardi was born in Graz in 1850, the son of Italian immigrants. He began working as an itinerant locksmith, but soon turned to the stage, acting in provincial theaters. He was discovered in 1870 and became one of the most popular actors in Vienna, so admired that the Viennese named one of their favorite dishes for him.

The Girardi-Rostbraten is accompanied by a light cream sauce scented with bay leaf and enriched with diced smoked ham and mushrooms. Serve with seasonal vegetables and buttered noodles. Open a bottle of Cabernet, Merlot, or Pinot Noir St.-Laurent.

About 1/2 cup clarified butter for sautéing
6 (7-ounce) slices of sirloin
6 tablespoons finely diced smoked ham
1 white onion, peeled and finely chopped
1/2 cup finely diced mushrooms
1/3 cup dry white wine
1 bay leaf
1/2 cup heavy cream
3/4 cup Brown Beef Stock (see Index)
1 tablespoon butter
1 teaspoon Dijon mustard
1/2 bunch parsley, finely chopped
1 tablespoon capers, drained
Salt and freshly ground white pepper to taste
Sour cream (optional, for a garnish)

1. Heat 1/3 cup clarified butter in a skillet and sauté the sirloin over medium-high heat until brown outside and medium-rare inside. Remove and set aside on a covered plate.

2. Degrease the skillet by wiping it out with a paper towel, add 2 tablespoons clarified butter, and sauté the smoked ham 2 to 3 minutes over medium-high heat. Add the onions and sauté until

golden. Add the mushrooms and sauté 4 to 5 minutes. Add the white wine and reduce almost all of the liquid.

3. Add the bay leaf, cream, and stock, and reduce to a sauce consistency. Swirl in the butter and whisk in the mustard. Do not allow the sauce to boil again or the mustard will have a bitter taste. Stir in the parsley, any meat juices from the covered plate, the capers, and salt and pepper to taste. Remove the bay leaf.

4. Place the meat on 6 warm plates, topped with the sauce. The dish may be garnished with sour cream piped through a pastry bag.

TAFELSPITZ

SERVES 6

Short ribs of beef are slowly simmered with a bouquet of vegetables to a special tenderness. Tafelspitz is a glory of Austrian cuisine, proving that simple, time-honored fare can be the most memorable. Because it requires little attention, practically cooking itself over a two- to three-hour period, Tafelspitz is well suited to both family dinners and entertaining. The succulent boiled beef is particularly wonderful served with its two traditional accompaniments, chive sauce and horseradish-apple sauce. The recipes for these fresh-tasting accents immediately follow the Tafelspitz. All that's needed for a perfect meal is buttered new potatoes with a sprinkling of dill and some creamed spinach. Any other creamed vegetable will be equally as good. It is interesting to note that the Viennese invariably serve a light white wine with this meat dish. We suggest a Pinot Blanc, Riesling, Chardonnay, or Sauvignon Blanc.

1 medium carrot
1 medium yellow turnip
1/2 celery root (celeriac)
1 celery stalk
1 medium onion
1 leek (both white and green parts), well rinsed and
    trimmed
1/2 bunch parsley
1 bay leaf
15 black peppercorns
4 pounds short ribs of beef with the bone (the meat on the
    bone should be 2 1/2 inches thick and not too fatty)

1. Peel the vegetables and cut them all into 1-inch slices.
2. Half fill a large pot with water and bring to a boil. Add the vegetables and seasonings and bring to a second boil.
3. Add the beef, lower the flame, and slowly simmer for 2 to 3 hours, until the meat is tender.
4. When the meat is done, remove the bone and carve against the grain into thick slices.

TRADITIONAL SAUCES FOR
THE TAFELSPITZ

CHIVE SAUCE

MAKES 3 CUPS

Yolks of 6 hard-cooked eggs
1/4 cup milk
5 slices of white bread without the crusts
1 cup mayonnaise
1/2 cup sour cream
1/3 cup white vinegar (about)
Salt and freshly ground white pepper to taste
3 bunches of chives, finely chopped (about 1/4 cup
chopped)

1. In a blender or food processor, combine the egg yolks, milk, and bread until smooth.

2. Stir in the mayonnaise and sour cream. Add white vinegar to taste and season with salt and pepper to taste. Stir in the chives.

3. Serve in a bowl to accompany the Tafelspitz.

HORSERADISH-APPLE SAUCE

MAKES 3 CUPS

6 apples, peeled, halved, and cored
1 whole clove
1/2 cup dry white wine
12 tablespoons freshly grated horseradish
Juice of 1 lemon
1 tablespoon sugar

1. Cook the apples in 3 cups of water with the clove and white wine until tender.
2. Refresh the apples in ice water and then smash to a mousse.
3. Stir in the horseradish, lemon juice, and sugar.
4. Serve in a bowl to accompany the Tafelspitz.

VIENNESE ROAST TENDERLOIN OF BEEF IN CREAM SAUCE

SERVES 6

We find that larding makes this beef even more succulent and tender. Capers add a special note to the smooth cream sauce. Serve with seasonal vegetables and lightly buttered noodles.

1 1/2 pounds whole tenderloin of beef, with fat removed
4 ounces fatback (bacon fat), cut into strips (1/2 cup cut up)
1 cup sour cream
1 tablespoon Dijon mustard
1 tablespoon capers, drained
Dash of dried thyme
Juice of 1 lemon
1/2 cup butter for frying
1 medium onion, diced
1 cup heavy cream
2 cups Brown Beef Stock (see Index)
Salt and freshly ground white pepper to taste

1. Preheat the oven to 400° F.

2. Lard the tenderloin by making small lengthwise incisions in the beef and inserting the strips of fatback.

3. In a bowl, mix the sour cream, mustard, capers, thyme, and lemon juice.

4. Heat 1/2 cup butter in a skillet and brown the tenderloin over medium-high heat on both sides. Transfer to a roasting pan and place in the oven for 25 minutes.

5. Meanwhile, fry the onion in the same skillet until golden. Add the heavy cream, bring to a boil, and reduce by half. Add the beef stock and again reduce by half.

6. Remove from the heat and stir in the sour cream mixture. Season with salt and pepper to taste and set aside.

7. Remove the beef from the oven and carve against the grain into 1-inch slices. Pour the sauce on 6 warm plates and arrange 2 slices of beef on the sauce for each serving.

FILET MIGNON WITH BEAUJOLAIS SAUCE AND A VARIETY OF MARINATED MUSHROOMS

SERVES 6

The supreme flavor of forest mushrooms gives this otherwise traditional dish a lavish distinction. A tip for preparation: instead of adding garlic directly to the mushroom assortment and overpowering its aroma, spear whole garlic cloves and stir them through the mushrooms for a few minutes. Perfect with Potato Strudel (see Index). The same fine Beaujolais used for cooking should accompany the dish at table.

1 tablespoon butter, plus about 1/2 cup for sautéing
2 medium onions, thinly sliced
1/2 cup Beaujolais
1¼ cups Brown Beef Stock (see Index)
6 black peppercorns
2 bay leaves
1/4 cup sliced fresh shiitake mushrooms
1/4 cup fresh enoki mushrooms (tiny Japanese mushrooms)
1/4 cup fresh chanterelles, rinsed, dried on paper towels,
    and torn in half by hand
4 shallots, peeled and minced
Pinch of dried thyme
2 garlic cloves, peeled
1 tablespoon tarragon vinegar
Salt and freshly ground white pepper to taste
6 (6-ounce) filet mignons
1/3 cup oil for sautéing

1. Heat 1/3 cup butter in a saucepan and brown the sliced onions over medium heat.

2. Add the Beaujolais, bring to a boil, and reduce almost all of the liquid.

3. Add the beef stock, peppercorns, and bay leaves, and reduce by half. Strain and keep warm.

4. Heat 2 tablespoons butter in a skillet over medium heat

and brown all of the mushrooms. Add the shallots and brown.

5. Add the thyme. Spear the garlic cloves on a kitchen fork and stir in the pan for 2 to 3 minutes.

6. Add the tarragon vinegar and salt and pepper to taste. Remove from the heat and allow the mushrooms to marinate while you prepare the filets.

7. Preheat the oven to 400° F.

8. Sprinkle the filets with salt and pepper.

9. Pour 1/3 cup oil in a large ovenproof skillet and heat well. Sauté the filets over medium-high heat on both sides to sear the meat, then finish cooking them in the oven for 6 to 8 minutes, in the same skillet.

10. While the filets are in the oven, bring the sauce to a boil once more and swirl in the 1 tablespoon butter. Heat the mushrooms through a second time.

11. Pour the sauce onto 6 warm plates and place the filets in the center, surrounded by marinated mushrooms.

LAMB FILLETS WITH MINT SAUCE

SERVES 6

Our interpretation of a classic marriage of flavors. We enhance our choice fillets with a sauce that sparkles with the fragrance of fresh mint leaves and a hint of mint liqueur. An impressive Easter dish! Wild rice and a full-bodied, elegant red wine are appropriate.

About 3/4 cup clarified butter for sautéing
12 lamb fillets, about 1 inch thick
6 shallots, peeled and finely diced
Leaves of 1 bunch fresh peppermint (about 1 cup) (reserve
    some nice leaves for garnishing each plate)
2 cloves garlic, chopped
2 tablespoons dry red wine
2 tablespoons clear mint liqueur (try a peppermint
    schnapps)
3/4 cup Lamb Stock (see Index)
Pinch of dried thyme
Salt and freshly ground white pepper to taste

1. Heat 1/3 cup clarified butter in a skillet and sauté 6 of the lamb fillets over medium-high heat on both sides until they are browned outside and pink inside. Remove and keep warm on a covered plate. Add another 1/3 cup clarified butter and repeat with the remaining fillets.

2. Heat 2 tablespoons clarified butter in the skillet and sauté the shallots over medium heat for 3 to 4 minutes, until they are transparent. Next add the mint leaves and garlic. Sauté 3 to 4 minutes.

3. Add the red wine and mint liqueur. Reduce almost all of the liquid.

4. Add the lamb stock and reduce to a sauce consistency.

5. Strain the sauce. Season with the thyme and salt and pepper to taste.

6. Slice the lamb fillets diagonally against the grain. Pour the sauce onto 6 warm plates. Arrange the slices of lamb in a circular pattern over the sauce. Garnish with mint leaves in the center. Arrange seasonal vegetables around the meat.

LAMB CUTLETS WITH POMMERY
MUSTARD SAUCE

SERVES 6

A simple harmony of lamb, tomatoes, and zucchini, vibrant in a pool of richly scented Pommery mustard sauce. A fine way to celebrate spring. Serve with a light salad, mushrooms, and crusty bread.

1¹/₂ cups olive oil for sautéing
24 lamb cutlets (4 per person)
8 shallots, peeled and finely diced
¹/₂ cup dry red wine
1 clove garlic, peeled and crushed
1 cup Lamb Stock (see Index) or Brown Veal Stock (see Index)
10 black peppercorns
1 bay leaf
1 tablespoon Pommery mustard
1 cup (2 sticks) butter
2 pinches of dried thyme
Salt and freshly ground white pepper to taste
3 medium zucchini, sliced à la julienne, into thin strips (about 4 cups sliced)
2 tomatoes, skin and seeds removed, and diced

1. Heat ¹/₄ cup olive oil in a skillet and sauté the lamb cutlets, 6 at a time, on both sides over medium-high heat, until brown outside and pink inside. Remove and keep warm on a covered plate. Repeat with the remaining cutlets, heating ¹/₄ cup oil for each batch.

2. Add the shallots to the skillet and sauté until golden. Add the red wine and garlic and reduce almost all of the liquid. Add the lamb stock, peppercorns, and bay leaf. Reduce to a sauce consistency.

3. Strain the sauce into another pan. Slowly whisk in the Pommery mustard. Over a very low flame, swirl in the butter. Do not allow the sauce to boil again. Add a pinch of thyme and season with salt and pepper to taste.

4. Heat 1/2 cup olive oil in a skillet and sauté the zucchini briefly over medium-high heat, about 1 minute. Add the tomato and again sauté briefly until tender. Season with a pinch of thyme.

5. Place 4 cutlets on each plate in a circular pattern. Pour the sauce in the middle and arrange the vegetables over the sauce.

LOIN OF LAMB WITH FOREST MUSHROOMS AND BASIL LEAVES

SERVES 6

Individual portions of lamb are browned, accented with a medley of sautéed forest mushrooms, and rolled in aromatic basil leaves. Each portion is then sealed in caul fat and quickly roasted to a mouth-watering succulence. The dish receives a Mediterranean accent from a flavorsome sauce of garlic and black olives. Unsurpassed served with Zucchini Tartlets (see Index). We suggest a bottle of Robert Mondavi's Cabernet Sauvignon.

1¹/₃ cups olive oil for sautéing
³/₄ cup fresh chanterelles, rinsed, dried on paper towels, and torn in half by hand
³/₄ cup fresh cepes, rinsed, drained, patted dry with paper towels, and cut in thin slices
¹/₂ cup fresh shiitake, thinly sliced
¹/₂ cup fresh pleurots, thinly sliced
8 shallots, peeled and finely diced
Pinch of dried thyme
4 cloves garlic, peeled
2 pounds boned loin of lamb, fat removed, cut into 6 portions
Salt and freshly ground white pepper to taste
12 large fresh basil leaves
¹/₂ pound caul fat
24 pitted black olives, finely diced, plus 2 tablespoons olive juice
1 cup Lamb Stock (see Index)

1. Preheat the oven to 425° F.

2. Heat ½ cup olive oil in a skillet and sauté all of the mushrooms over medium-high heat for 7 to 8 minutes. Add half of the shallots and sauté until golden. Add a pinch of thyme.

3. Spear the garlic cloves on a kitchen fork and stir through the mushrooms for 2 minutes. Reserve the garlic. Remove the mushrooms and shallots and allow to cool.

4. Heat ½ cup olive oil in the same skillet. Sprinkle the meat with salt and pepper to taste. Quickly brown the meat over medium-high heat for about 1 minute on each side. Remove and allow to cool.

5. Place some mushrooms over each portion of lamb and top with 2 basil leaves. Seal each portion in caul fat by wrapping it like a present, tucking the fat under each end securely.

6. Heat ⅓ cup olive oil in an ovenproof skillet and sauté the prepared meat over medium-high heat for 1 minute on each side. Transfer the skillet to the oven and roast for 3 to 4 minutes. Keep warm on a covered plate.

7. In the skillet in which the lamb has been roasted, add the remaining shallots and sauté over medium-high heat until golden. Add the whole garlic and brown. Add the sliced olives and olive juice and reduce almost all of the liquid. Add the lamb stock and reduce by half. Remove the garlic.

8. Cut each portion of lamb into 5 slices. Arrange the slices on warm plates. Pour the sauce over the meat.

PORK MEDALLIONS IN SORREL SAUCE

SERVES 6

The light tanginess of fresh sorrel is a great complement for pork. Fast, easy, and delicious—we particularly like this dish served with Truffle Crepes (see Index) and a fresh vegetable.

1 cup plus 2 tablespoons clarified butter for sautéing
2 pounds trimmed pork tenderloin, cut into 18 medallions
    (3 per person)
4 shallots, peeled and finely diced
2 garlic cloves, peeled
1/3 cup red wine vinegar
1 bunch sorrel, rinsed, dried, and finely chopped (a scant
    1/2 cup)
1 cup heavy cream
4 tablespoons Pork Stock (see Index)
1 tablespoon butter
Salt and freshly ground white pepper to taste
1/2 bunch sorrel, rinsed, drained, and finely sliced for
    garnishing (a scant 1/4 cup)

1. Heat 1/3 cup clarified butter in a skillet and sauté the medallions of pork in batches of 6, adding 1/3 cup butter for each batch. Cook over medium-high heat for 3 to 4 minutes on each side. Remove and keep warm on a covered plate.

2. Degrease the skillet by wiping it out with a paper towel and heat 2 tablespoons fresh clarified butter. Add the shallots and garlic cloves and sauté over medium-high heat until golden. Add the red wine vinegar and reduce by half.

3. Add the chopped sorrel and heavy cream. Again reduce by half.

4. Add the pork stock and allow to reduce for 4 to 5 minutes. Strain the sauce into another skillet and swirl in the butter. Season with salt and white pepper to taste.

5. Place the pork medallions on warm plates and pour some sauce over them. Arrange the sliced sorrel near the medallions.

PORK CHOPS WITH CAPER SAUCE

SERVES 6

Capers add zest to these juicy garlic-studded pork chops. An easy, last-minute dish. Serve with string beans and Lyonnaise Potatoes (see Index). Any dry, light California Chardonnay goes well with pork.

1 garlic clove, peeled
1/2 cup olive oil, plus 2/3 cup olive oil for sautéing
12 (4–5-ounce) pork chops
2 teaspoons dry red wine
1 cup Pork Stock (see Index)
Juice of 1 lemon
1/4 cup heavy cream
2 tablespoons capers, drained
Dash of caper juice
1/2 bunch fresh parsley, chopped
Salt and freshly ground white pepper to taste

1. Pass the garlic clove through a garlic press, then mix with the 1/2 cup olive oil, or process together until smooth.

2. Brush the pork chops on both sides with the garlic-oil mixture.

3. Heat 1/3 cup oil in a skillet over medium-high heat and sauté 6 of the chops for about 5 to 6 minutes on each side. Lift out the chops, drain, and keep warm on a covered plate. Add another 1/3 cup oil and repeat with the remaining chops.

4. Degrease the skillet by wiping it out with a paper towel. Add the red wine and stock. Reduce to a sauce consistency. Add the lemon juice and cream. Strain the sauce and return to the pan. Add the capers and a dash of caper juice. Stir in the parsley. Season with salt and pepper to taste.

5. Arrange the chops on 6 warm plates and spoon the sauce over them.

BRAISED PORK FILLETS IN WHITE CABBAGE

SERVES 6

Cabbage leaves are layered with a rich mushroom mousse and then rolled around juicy fillets from the pork tenderloin. Braising with an assortment of vegetables gives depth of flavor. This is somewhat complicated but is especially rewarding on a chill winter's night.

6 (8-ounce) pork fillets (from the tenderloin), trimmed of all fat
Salt and freshly ground black pepper to taste
Vegetable oil
2 cloves garlic, peeled and crushed
1 medium onion, sliced
1/2 large carrot, peeled and diced
1/4 celery root (celeriac), diced
A few stems of parsley
1 medium head white cabbage
1 tablespoon caraway seed
1 bay leaf
White peppercorns
Dash of white vinegar
1/3 cup olive oil for sautéing
1/2 pound bacon, chopped
1/2 cup dry white wine
1/2 cup Pork Stock (see Index)
1/2 cup Bouillon (see Index)

MUSHROOM MOUSSE
1 pound white mushrooms, cleaned and chopped
10 shallots, peeled and chopped
4 tablespoons butter
2 cloves garlic, peeled and minced
Juice of 1 lemon
1 cup heavy cream
1 egg yolk
Salt and freshly ground white pepper to taste

1. Season the pork fillets with salt and pepper. Place them in a pan, cover with oil, and cover with layers of the garlic, vegetables, and parsley. Cover and allow to marinate for 12 hours.

2. Take off 8–10 large leaves from the cabbage and reserve. Chop the rest of the leaves and set aside. Discard the core.

3. Bring 1 quart of water to a boil. Add the caraway, bay leaf, peppercorns, and vinegar.

4. Blanch the 8–10 large cabbage leaves, remove, and refresh in ice water. Drain the cabbage leaves on paper towels.

5. For the mousse, sauté the mushrooms and shallots in the butter over medium heat. When the shallots are golden, add the garlic. Add the lemon juice and cream.

6. Puree in a food processor and return to the pan. Bring to a boil and reduce to a firm consistency.

7. Remove from the heat, stir in the egg yolk, season with salt and pepper to taste, and allow to cool.

8. Preheat the oven to 300° F.

9. Remove the meat from the marinade and let the oil drip off. Strain the vegetables from the marinade and set aside.

10. Heat 1/3 cup oil in a skillet and sauté the fillets over high heat until golden on both sides. Remove and allow to cool.

11. Spread out the large cabbage leaves and cover with mushroom mousse. Place the fillets on top and roll up the cabbage leaves. Tie tightly with kitchen twine.

12. Over medium-high heat, sauté the chopped bacon for 4 to 5 minutes in a large ovenproof cooking pot with a lid. Add the vegetables and chopped cabbage from the marinade and sauté for 4 to 5 minutes. Pour in the white wine and layer the fillets over the vegetables. Cover with the pork stock and bouillon. Cover the pot and place it in the preheated oven. Braise for 40 minutes.

13. Remove the fillets. Reduce the remaining stock to a sauce consistency and strain it.

14. Slice each fillet of pork and arrange it in a circular pattern on an individual plate. Place the vegetables alongside and drizzle the sauce over all.

MEDALLIONS OF PORK WITH
A DARK BEER AND CARAWAY SAUCE

SERVES 6

An intensely flavorful dish with an aromatic, slowly simmered sauce. If you wish, marinate the pork overnight. Serve this robust winter fare with String Beans with Bacon (see Index). Accompany with the same dark beer used for cooking.

2 cloves garlic, peeled
2 cups olive oil
6 (7-ounce) tenderloins of pork, cut into 18 medallions (3
    per person) (reserve trimmed fat and meat for making
    the sauce; cut the trimmings into 1-inch cubes)
1 medium carrot, peeled and finely diced
1 celery root (celeriac), finely diced
1 celery stalk, finely diced
1 medium onion, finely diced
Caraway seed
1 (12-ounce) bottle dark beer
1/4 cup Pork Stock (see Index)
Salt and freshly ground white pepper to taste

1. Process the garlic cloves with the olive oil until smooth.

2. Place the pork medallions in a pan, cover with the garlic oil, and add the vegetables and a sprinkling of caraway seed. Cover and allow to marinate 12 hours or overnight.

3. Sauté the reserved cubed meat and fat in a skillet. Add the vegetables from the marinade and sauté. Add the dark beer and reduce by half. Season with caraway seed to taste. Add 1/4 cup water and the stock and simmer, uncovered, over low heat for 1 1/2 hours.

4. Remove the medallions from the marinade and pat them dry. Brush them on both sides with the garlic oil preparation. Heat the remaining garlic oil in a skillet and sauté the medallions over medium-high heat for 3 to 4 minutes on each side. Remove and set aside on a covered plate.

5. Degrease the skillet by wiping it out with a paper towel. Strain the sauce into the skillet, add the pork medallions, and heat through without allowing the sauce to boil.

6. Arrange the medallions on 6 plates and spoon sauce over each.

CHAPTER 9

Vegetables and Side Dishes

The best side dishes are often the simplest—a colorful array of fresh vegetables, a fine salad, molded white or wild rice. There are times, however, when you will want to complete your meal with something a little more special. Here we give the potato, well loved in Austria, particular attention. This simple vegetable is subject to ingenious transformations, making it compatible with dishes ranging from the unassuming to the elegant. Inexpensive and surprisingly nutritious, the potato can be enjoyed in many delectable guises.

POTATO STRUDEL

SERVES 6

Golden pastry enfolds a savory mixture of potatoes, onions, marjoram, and cream. Served with a good soup, this side dish becomes a rich, earthy meal in itself.

1 pound Idaho potatoes
Vegetable oil for greasing the baking sheet
12 ounces puff pastry (readymade is acceptable)
1/3 cup olive oil for sautéing
1 pound onions, finely sliced
1 clove garlic, peeled
Dash of marjoram
Salt and freshly ground white pepper to taste
2 egg yolks mixed with a few drops of water
1/4 cup heavy cream

1. Peel the potatoes and cut into finger-thick slices. Soak the slices in cold water.

2. Preheat the oven to 400° F. Grease a baking sheet with oil.

3. Roll out the puff pastry to 1/4 inch thick. Cut into 2 pieces, one slightly larger than the other. Place the smaller half on the baking sheet.

4. Heat 1/3 cup olive oil in a skillet, add the onions, and sauté over medium-high heat until golden. Drain the potatoes, add them, and stir for 3 minutes. Spear the garlic clove on a kitchen fork and stir it through the mixture for 1 minute. Season with marjoram, salt, and white pepper to taste. Remove from the heat and allow to cool to room temperature.

5. Spread the mixture on the pastry bottom, leaving 1 inch free on all sides. Brush the sides with egg yolk, cover with the larger sheet of pastry, and seal. Brush the pastry top with the remaining egg yolk.

6. Bake the potato strudel for 15 minutes. Remove from the oven and let it cool for 5 minutes on the baking sheet. Cut a 1-inch-thick strip of dough from the top of the strudel and pour in the cream.

7. Lower the oven to 200° F. (WARM) and bake the strudel for another 10 minutes, to allow the cream to thicken.

8. Remove, slice, and serve warm.

SCALLION POTATOES

SERVES 6

Mashed potatoes and sautéed scallions are mixed, shaped into flavorsome little nuggets, and sautéed to golden perfection. This delicious and original side dish can be served with a wide variety of meats and poultry.

1 pound Idaho potatoes, peeled
1 egg yolk
Dash of ground nutmeg
Salt and freshly ground white pepper to taste
1 bunch scallions (white portion only), sliced
1/3 cup butter for sautéing
1 tablespoon olive oil for sautéing

1. Preheat the oven to 200° F. (WARM).

2. In a pot of cold water, bring the potatoes to a boil, cook until tender, and then mash them.

3. Place the mashed potatoes in an ovenproof pot over low heat. Stir in the egg yolk. Season with nutmeg, salt, and pepper. Transfer the pot to the oven for 10 minutes.

4. Over medium heat, sauté the scallions in butter for 4 to 5 minutes and mix them into the potatoes. Form little cylinders or ovals.

5. Heat the olive oil in a skillet and sauté the scallion potatoes over medium-high heat until golden on all sides.

6. Drain on paper towels and serve warm with a grinding of fresh pepper.

DUCHESSE POTATOES

SERVES 6

All you need is a pastry bag to make these delicate potato rosettes—a simple and elegant dish.

1¹/₂ pounds Idaho potatoes
2 egg yolks
Salt and freshly ground white pepper to taste
¹/₄ teaspoon ground nutmeg
Butter

1. Quarter the potatoes (unpeeled) and boil until tender. Allow to cool, peel, and mash the potatoes.

2. Preheat the oven to 200° F. (WARM).

3. Mix the mashed potatoes and 1 of the egg yolks. Season with salt, pepper, and the nutmeg. Place the mixture in the oven for 10 minutes. Remove.

4. Preheat the oven to 400° F.

5. Grease a baking sheet with butter. Place the potato mixture in a pastry bag fitted with a large rosette tip and squeeze 3-inch-high rosette swirls onto the baking sheet. Beat the remaining egg yolk with a few drops of water and brush the top of each rosette with it. Bake for 5 minutes, until the tops are browned.

TRUFFLE CREPES

SERVES 6

An inventive marriage of the faithful potato and the elegant truffle. A worldly indulgence.

1 pound Idaho potatoes
1 egg yolk
Salt and freshly ground white pepper to taste
1 tablespoon butter for sautéing
3 shallots, peeled and finely diced
1 tablespoon black truffles, finely diced
1 tablespoon truffle juice
1/3 cup olive oil for sautéing

1. Quarter the unpeeled potatoes, and boil until tender. Allow to cool, then peel and mash.
2. Preheat the oven to 200° F. (WARM).
3. Combine the mashed potatoes and egg yolk. Season with salt and pepper. Place the mixture in the oven for 10 minutes.
4. Meanwhile, melt the butter in a skillet and sauté the shallots over medium-high heat for 4 to 5 minutes. Stir in the truffles and add the truffle juice. Reduce by half.
5. Stir the shallots and truffles into the potatoes. Form 12 flat oval crepe shapes. Heat the olive oil in a skillet and sauté the crepes over medium-high heat until golden.
6. Serve warm.

ROSTI POTATOES

SERVES 6

A crisp, golden combination of potatoes and onions, this hearty dish makes a great brunch addition to fluffy scrambled eggs.

1 pound Idaho potatoes
1/4 cup vegetable oil
1 medium onion, chopped
Salt and freshly ground white pepper to taste
1/4 cup finely chopped parsley for garnishing

1. Boil the potatoes in their skins for 20 minutes. Peel them and grate them coarsely.

2. Heat the oil in a large skillet until very hot.

3. Add the onion and cook over medium heat until golden.

4. Sprinkle the potatoes over the onions, cover the skillet, and cook 10 minutes, shaking the skillet occasionally.

5. Turn the potato-onion pancake in one piece: cover the skillet with a platter and flip them over together so the pancake comes out whole on the plate. Slide the pancake back into the skillet, brown side up. Cover and cook another 10 minutes, until crisp.

6. Garnish with the chopped parsley and serve.

A brief simmering in veal stock gives a rewarding flavor to Château and Lyonnaise potatoes.

CHÂTEAU POTATOES

SERVES 6

A simple yet special dish that derives its name from the square château-like shapes of the potatoes.

18 small red-skinned potatoes
1/3 cup vegetable oil
1/4 cup Brown Veal Stock (see Index)

1. Turn the potatoes against a sharp paring knife, faceting them into 6-sided cylinders.
2. Blanch the potatoes in boiling water and drain. Heat the oil in a large skillet and fry the potatoes over medium heat until brown.
3. Remove the potatoes from the oil and place in a saucepan with the stock. Cook over medium heat until the liquid is reduced by half, about 7 to 8 minutes.
4. Cover and keep warm until ready to serve.

LYONNAISE POTATOES

SERVES 6

A variation on the preceding recipe, these potatoes are touched with a hint of garlic, as well as the traditional onions.

1 pound potatoes
1/4 cup olive oil for sautéing
1 pound onions, sliced
Dash of thyme
1 clove garlic, peeled
1/4 cup Brown Veal Stock (see Index)

1. Boil the potatoes in their skins for about 15 minutes. Allow to cool, then peel and cut into 2-inch-thick slices.
2. In a large skillet, heat the oil over medium heat and sauté the onions until golden. Slowly stir in the potatoes and sprinkle with the thyme. Spear the garlic clove on a kitchen fork and stir through the mixture several times. Cook for 10 minutes, until the potatoes form a golden crust.
3. Pour in the veal stock, heat through, and serve.

*Two Palatschinke
variations: Apricot and
Farmer Cheese*

Salmon Steak with Shrimp
Ragout

Three Tagliatelle:
(from top) Smoked Salmon
and Green Peas;
Mussels, Clams, and
Carrots; Lobster, Shrimp,
and Crayfish

Escallopes of Venison with
Lentils and Chanterelles

*Warm Chocolate
Almond Cake with
Piped Whipped Cream*

Soft-Shell Crabs
with Almond Sauce (top)
and Langoustines in
Pernod Ginger Sauce

Calf's Head in Aspic with
Red Onion Vinaigrette
(Headcheese)

Salzburger Nockerl
(Vanilla Soufflé)

POTATO NOODLES

SERVES 6

Austrians living abroad sigh with remembered pleasure at the mention of potato noodles, a beloved regional specialty of Styria and Tyrol. Try these once and you will share the enthusiasm. A great complement for meat dishes.

1 pound Idaho potatoes
3/4 cup flour
1 egg
1/2 teaspoon ground nutmeg
1/8 teaspoon salt
1/3 cup olive oil for sautéing

1. Boil the unpeeled potatoes until tender and refrigerate overnight. The next day, peel the potatoes and force them through a fine sieve.

2. Mix the sieved potatoes, flour, and egg to form a dough. Season with the nutmeg and salt. Roll the dough into a finger-thick cylindrical shape and cut it into inch-long sections. Roll each section into noodles thick in the middle and tapering at the ends.

3. Bring 2 quarts of water to a boil. Add the noodles and simmer for about 5 minutes, until the noodles rise to the surface. Remove the noodles with a slotted spoon and refresh in ice water.

4. Heat the olive oil in a skillet and sauté the potato noodles over medium-high heat until golden brown.

POTATO CROQUETTES ROLLED IN ALMONDS

SERVES 6

A variation on the familiar croquettes, these potatoes are rolled in ground almonds rather than bread crumbs. This superb contrast of texture is incredibly delicious!

1 pound Idaho potatoes, peeled
1 egg yolk
Salt and freshly ground white pepper to taste
Flour
2 eggs mixed with 1/4 cup milk
1/2 cup ground blanched almonds
Oil for deep frying

1. Cook the potatoes in boiling, salted water until tender. Allow them to cool and mash them.
2. Preheat the oven to 200° F. (WARM).
3. Mix the mashed potatoes and the egg yolk. Season with salt and pepper. Place in the oven for 10 minutes. Allow to cool.
4. Form the potato mixture into 2-inch cylinders. Roll in the flour, dip in the egg-milk mixture, and then roll in the almonds. Deep-fry in very hot oil until golden brown.

SIMPLE POTATO CROQUETTES

These are prepared in the same way as the above recipe, substituting bread crumbs for the almonds.

POTATO ROULADE

SERVES 6

Beautiful when sliced, our roulade holds a luscious mixture of sautéed ham, shallots, mushrooms, and fragrant basil. Unsurpassed with game, or a hearty meal in itself (serving four) with a good glass of wine.

1 pound potatoes, unpeeled
1 egg
1 cup flour, plus flour for rolling out dough
1 tablespoon butter
4 shallots, peeled and diced
1/2 cup finely diced cooked ham
1/2 cup diced mushrooms
2 tablespoons finely chopped basil
2 tablespoons olive oil
Salt and freshly ground white pepper to taste

1. Boil the unpeeled potatoes until tender. Allow to cool, peel, and mash.

2. Mix the mashed potatoes, egg, and flour to form a dough. Allow to rest for 15 minutes.

3. Heat the butter in a skillet and sauté the shallots, ham, mushrooms, and basil. Allow to cool.

4. Sprinkle flour on a tabletop and roll out the dough into a 1/2-inch-thick square. Cover with the cooled ham mixture, leaving 1 inch uncovered on all sides. Roll the dough and carefully seal the ends by pinching and twisting the dough.

5. Roll the roulade in buttered baking parchment cut 4 inches longer than the roulade. Tie the ends of the parchment with kitchen twine. Place the roulade in a pot of boiling water and simmer, uncovered, for 20 minutes.

6. Take out the roulade, refresh in ice water, and remove the parchment. Cut the roulade into 1/2-inch slices.

7. Heat the olive oil in a skillet and gently sauté the roulade until golden on all sides.

SPAETZLE

SERVES 6

Spaetzle are wonderful for absorbing rich sauces and can be served with almost any sauced dish. Spaetzle are considered the pasta of central Europe, a mainstay of Austrian meals.

2 cups flour
1/2 cup milk
3 eggs, beaten
Salt and freshly ground white pepper to taste
4 tablespoons butter

1. Mix the flour, milk, and eggs to form a dough.
2. Season with salt and pepper and process in a spaetzle machine.* If you don't wish to purchase a spaetzle machine, you can try pushing the spaetzle dough through the coarsest side of a four-sided grater. Set the grater over a plate and "grate" a piece of dough the size of your fist. Repeat with the remaining dough.
3. Bring a large pot of water to a boil. Drop in the spaetzle and return to a boil. Remove the spaetzle and refresh in ice water. Drain and pat dry with paper towels.
4. Sauté the spaetzle in the butter in a large skillet over medium-high heat without browning, for 4 to 5 minutes.
5. Serve immediately.

* A spaetzle machine looks like a large cheese grater. These machines can be found at most gourmet shops and are inexpensive.

DUMPLINGS IN A NAPKIN
Serviettenknödel

SERVES 6

Knödel, or dumplings, are a popular side dish in Austria. Try this sophisticated variation cooked in a white linen napkin.

15 stale dinner rolls
2 cups milk
3 eggs, separated, at room temperature
8 tablespoons butter, melted, plus butter to grease the
    napkin
Salt and freshly ground white pepper to taste
1/4 teaspoon ground nutmeg
4 tablespoons olive oil for sautéing

1. Remove the crusts from the rolls and cut the inside of the rolls into 1-inch cubes. There should be about 8 cups cubed. Soak the cubed bread in the milk.

2. In an electric blender, beat the egg yolks and the melted butter until frothy. Stir this mixture into the rolls and milk. Season with salt and pepper to taste and the nutmeg.

3. Beat the egg whites until stiff peaks form and carefully fold into the bread mixture.

4. Bring a large pot of water to a boil. Spread out a white linen napkin and grease it lightly with butter. Form the bread mixture into a 5-inch-thick cylinder and place it on the lower end of the napkin. Roll up the napkin and tie the ends securely with string.

5. Place the napkin in the boiling water and simmer for 25 minutes. Refresh in ice water, untie, and slice the dumpling. Discard the end slices.

6. Heat the olive oil in a skillet and sauté the dumplings over medium-high heat for 1 to 2 minutes on each side before serving.

MUSHROOM RICE

SERVES 6

This easy favorite with limitless possibilities is equally at home with a simple baked chicken, a delicate Naturschnitzel (see Index), or hearty meat.

4 tablespoons butter
1 onion, finely diced
1/2 pound mushrooms, cleaned and sliced (about 2 cups sliced)
2 cups Bouillon (see Index) or Chicken Stock (see Index)
1 cup raw rice
Salt and freshly ground black pepper to taste
1/2 bunch parsley, finely chopped

1. Heat the butter in a large saucepan and sauté the onion until transparent. Add the mushrooms, and sauté.

2. Pour in the bouillon, stir in the rice, cover, and cook over low heat for 20 minutes.

3. Uncover and continue cooking for 5 minutes. Season with salt and pepper to taste. Sprinkle with the parsley.

BROCCOLI FLAN

SERVES 6

A delicate, vibrant, and easy accompaniment for veal or seafood. Wonderful served alone as a light vegetarian supper dish for two.

2 teaspoons butter, plus butter to grease the baking cups
1¹/2 pounds fresh broccoli
1 egg
1/3 cup heavy cream
Salt and freshly ground white pepper to taste
Dash of ground nutmeg

1. Preheat the oven to 325° F. Grease 6 individual ovenproof cups with butter.

2. Cook the broccoli in boiling salted water until tender. Drain and puree in a blender or food processor with the egg, cream, and 2 teaspoons of butter. Season with salt, pepper, and nutmeg to taste.

3. Fill the greased cups with the broccoli mousse. Place the cups in a roasting pan and pour warm water into the pan until it comes halfway up the cups. Poach in the oven for 50 minutes.

4. Serve as quickly as possible.

CHAMPAGNE CABBAGE

SERVES 6

Champagne gives a light, fresh sparkle to white cabbage. In Viennese cuisine, this is a traditional accompaniment for poultry and game.

6 tablespoons butter
2 medium onions, finely sliced
1 teaspoon caraway seed
1 medium head white cabbage, rinsed, cored, and sliced
    into thin strips
1 teaspoon sugar
1/4 cup white wine vinegar
1 cup champagne
1/2 cup heavy cream
Salt and freshly ground white pepper to taste

1. Melt 4 tablespoons of the butter in a tall pot and sauté the onions and caraway seed over medium-high heat for 4 to 5 minutes.

2. Add the cabbage slices and sauté for about 3 minutes.

3. Stir in the sugar. Add the vinegar and champagne. Bring to a boil and reduce until there is very little liquid left.

4. Stir in the cream, the remaining 2 tablespoons butter, and salt and pepper to taste.

5. Serve on the plate or as a side dish.

VIENNESE RED CABBAGE

SERVES 6

A fragrant companion to duck, game birds, and pork. To give this cabbage a special sweet-tartness, you may sprinkle in some lingonberries after cooking.

1/2 **cup vegetable oil**
1 **onin, finely sliced**
1 **medium head red cabbage, rinsed, cored, and sliced into**
    thin strips
1 **tablespoon sugar**
1 **cup dry red wine**
1 **bay leaf**
1/2 **stick cinnamon**
Salt and freshly ground white pepper to taste

1. Heat the oil in a tall pot and sauté the onion over medium-high heat until golden.
2. Add the cabbage and sauté for 4 to 5 minutes, stirring occasionally.
3. Stir in the sugar and allow to caramelize.
4. Pour in the red wine, add the bay leaf and cinnamon, and cook until tender. Season with salt and pepper.

GLAZED CUCUMBERS

SERVES 6

Elegant with salmon or lemon sole.

6 medium cucumbers
3 tablespoons butter
1/3 cup clear Chicken Stock (see Index) or Brown Veal Stock
   (see Index)
2 tablespoons chopped fresh dillweed
2 teaspoons sherry vinegar
Salt and freshly ground white pepper to taste

1. Peel the cucumbers, cut lengthwise, remove the seeds, and cut into 1/2-inch slices.

2. Melt the butter in a skillet. Add the cucumber slices, sauté for 4 to 5 minutes over medium-high heat, and add the stock. Simmer over low heat until the cucumber is tender but not too soft, about 5 minutes.

3. Stir in the dill and sherry vinegar, and season with salt and pepper to taste.

4. Serve as a side dish or on the plate with the main course.

ENDIVE IN CREAM

SERVES 6

4 medium endives, the cores removed, and cut into 1-inch-
    thick slices
1 tablespoon butter
4 shallots, peeled and finely diced
1/4 cup heavy cream
Juice of 1/2 lemon
Salt and freshly ground white pepper to taste

1. Blanch the endives in boiling salted water for 1 minute and
then refresh in ice water.
2. Heat the butter in a skillet, add the shallots, and cook over
low heat for 4 to 5 minutes, without browning. Add the cream and
reduce over low heat to a sauce consistency, about 5 minutes.
3. Add the endives and lemon juice. Heat through and season
with salt and pepper.
4. Serve as a side dish.

BRAISED FENNEL

SERVES 6

The anise flavor of fennel is perfect with fish.

Butter to grease the dish
3 medium heads fennel, cut in quarters lengthwise, then
    sliced at an angle into 1-inch-thick strips
1/2 cup Brown Veal Stock (see Index)
1 bay leaf
4–5 peppercorns

1. Preheat the oven to 350° F. Butter a baking dish.

2. Place the fennel in the baking dish. Pour in the stock. Add the bay leaf and peppercorns. Cover with aluminum foil and braise in the oven for 15 minutes.

3. Remove the fennel from its braising liquid and serve.

KOHLRABI GRATINÉ

SERVES 6

The kohlrabi, a special turnip-like root vegetable much loved in Austria, is widely available in American markets. The following dish goes particularly well with broiled meats.

6 (6-ounce) kohlrabi
2 tablespoons butter, plus butter to grease the dish
1/2 cup Brown Veal Stock (see Index)
1/4 cup heavy cream
1 egg yolk
Salt and freshly ground white pepper to taste
1 garlic clove, peeled

1. Peel the kohlrabi and cut into 1-inch-thick slices.

2. Heat the 2 tablespoons of butter in a skillet and sauté the kohlrabi for 3 to 4 minutes. Add the veal stock and simmer, uncovered, until the kohlrabi is partially done, about 25 minutes.

3. Butter an au gratin dish and preheat the broiler.

4. Beat the cream and egg yolk together and add to the kohlrabi. Reduce over a low flame for 5 minutes, to a sauce consistency. Remove from the heat and season with salt and pepper to taste.

5. Add the garlic clove, return to a simmer, and cook for 3 to 4 minutes. Remove the garlic.

6. Remove from the heat and transfer to the au gratin dish. Place under the broiler until browned and bubbly. Serve in the au gratin dish.

CREAMED SPINACH

SERVES 6

A traditional side dish for Tafelspitz, slowly simmered beef (see Index).

2 pounds spinach leaves, cleaned and the stems removed
3/4 cup Brown Veal Stock (see Index)
1/2 garlic clove, peeled
1 tablespoon butter
3 tablespoons flour
1/4 cup heavy cream
Salt and freshly ground white pepper to taste
1/4 teaspoon ground nutmeg, or to taste

1. Blanch the spinach in boiling salted water for 2 to 3 minutes. Drain.

2. Puree the spinach in a blender or food processor with the veal stock and garlic.

3. Heat the butter in a skillet. Remove from the heat and stir in the flour to make a roux.

4. Stir the spinach puree into the roux. Return the skillet to the flame and stir in the cream, bring quickly to a boil, and remove from the heat. Season with salt, pepper, and nutmeg to taste.

STRING BEANS WITH BACON

SERVES 6

An uncomplicated and attractive presentation.

1 pound string beans, rinsed, ends cut off
6 slices bacon
Salt and freshly ground white pepper to taste

1. Boil the beans in salted water until still crisp and refresh in ice water. Drain.

2. Made 6 bunches of the string beans and wrap with the bacon. In a large skillet, sauté the bacon-bean bundles for 2 to 3 minutes over a high flame.

3. Serve hot, sprinkled with salt and pepper.

STRING BEANS WITH DILL

SERVES 6

Veal stock and dill give the beans a rich and refreshing flavor. Delicious with meat or chicken.

1¹/₂ pounds string beans, tips removed
3 tablespoons butter
4 shallots, peeled and finely diced
¹/₄ cup or more Brown Veal Stock (see Index)
¹/₃ cup heavy cream
3 tablespoons chopped fresh dillweed
2 tablespoons red wine vinegar
Salt and freshly ground white pepper to taste

1. Cut the string beans into ¹/₂-inch pieces. Blanch in boiling salted water for 2 minutes. Refresh in ice water and set aside.

2. Heat the butter in a skillet and sauté the shallots over medium-high heat for 3 to 4 minutes.

3. Add ¹/₄ cup veal stock and the cream, bring to a boil, and reduce over low heat to a sauce consistency, about 5 minutes.

4. Add the string beans and simmer until tender. You may need to add more veal stock occasionally to maintain a sauce consistency.

5. When the beans are tender, stir in the chopped dill and vinegar. Season with salt and pepper to taste.

TOMATOES STUFFED WITH SPINACH

SERVES 6

A hint of nutmeg adds finesse to this versatile side dish for beef and pork.

2 tablespoons butter
1³/4 pounds spinach (leaves only), rinsed
Salt and freshly ground white pepper to taste
Dash of ground nutmeg
1 clove garlic, peeled
3 large tomatoes
3 tablespoons beef broth

1. Preheat the oven to 350° F.
2. Melt the butter in a skillet over medium-high heat, add the spinach leaves, cover, and allow to cook for a minute. Season with salt, pepper, nutmeg to taste. Remove from the flame.
3. Spear the garlic clove on a kitchen fork and stir it through the spinach several times. Allow the spinach to cool.
4. Blanch the tomatoes in boiling water, refresh in ice water, and peel. Cut each tomato in half and scoop out the seeds.
5. Stuff the spinach into the tomato halves. Pour the beef broth onto a small baking sheet and place the tomatoes on it. Heat through in the preheated oven for 2 to 3 minutes.

VEGETABLES PROVENÇALE

SERVES 6

This array of vegetables is spectacular served with red meats—beef, game, or lamb.

2 teaspoons butter
2 medium onions, thinly sliced
2 medium zucchini
1 medium eggplant, unpeeled
1 medium yellow squash
1/2 cup Brown Veal Stock (see Index) or 1/2 cup Bouillon
     (see Index)
Salt and freshly ground white pepper to taste

1. Preheat the oven to 325° F.
2. Heat the butter in a skillet and sauté the onions over medium-high heat until soft but not browned.
3. Cut the remaining vegetables in 1-inch-thick rounds. Cut the eggplant rounds into eighths.
4. Layer the onions on the bottom of a medium-sized roasting pan. Alternate layers of the other vegetables for a colorful effect.
5. Pour in the stock, cover with aluminum foil, and steam in the oven for 40 minutes.

ZUCCHINI TARTLETS

SERVES 6

This is our version of quiche and is excellent with poultry and game. The individual tartlets are a nice touch for presentation, or you can use one quiche pan. Served with a tomato salad and crisp white wine, this makes for a terrific summer lunch.

1 pound zucchini, cut à la julienne, into thin strips
1 teaspoon salt
Butter to grease pans
1/2 cup Swiss cheese, shredded
2 eggs, beaten
1 clove garlic, peeled and crushed
Dash of oregano
Salt and freshly ground white pepper to taste

SHORT PASTRY
1 cup sifted all-purpose flour
1/2 teaspoon salt
1/3 cup chilled lard
2–3 teaspoons ice water

1. Stir the flour and salt together in a bowl. Using two knives or a pastry cutter, cut the lard into the dry mixture until the mixture resembles a coarse meal.

2. Sprinkle 1 teaspoon of the ice water over the surface and mix it in quickly with a fork. Add more water as needed until the pastry just holds together. Do not overmix. Roll the pastry into a ball and use immediately, or wrap in plastic wrap and refrigerate until needed, up to 24 hours.

3. Place the julienned zucchini in a bowl, sprinkle with 1 teaspoon salt, and set aside.

4. Preheat the oven to 375° F.

5. Grease 6 round tartlet pans (2-inch diameter) or 1 (9-inch) quiche pan with butter.

6. Roll out the short pastry to 1/4 inch thick and mold the

dough in each tartlet pan, covering the bottom and sides completely. Prick the bottom and sides of the crust, then place some dried beans in each pan. Bake until the pastry is half done, about 10 minutes. Discard the beans and allow the crusts to cool.

7. Keep the oven at 375° F.

8. Squeeze the water from the zucchini and place it in a bowl with the cheese. Add the eggs, garlic, oregano, and salt and pepper to taste. Mix well. Fill each tartlet pan to the top with the zucchini mixture and bake for 12 to 15 minutes, until golden and crusty on top.

9. Remove the tartlets carefully from the pans and serve warm.

CHAPTER 10

Desserts

In 1683 the Turks abandoned a lengthy siege of Vienna, leaving behind their supply of coffee beans. Under the guidance of Georg Kolschitzky, a soldier of fortune familiar with Eastern ways, the Viennese were quickly initiated into the pleasures of a new beverage. The first Viennese coffeehouse was opened on January 12, 1685, and a way of life was born. An institution in Vienna, the coffeehouse is a salon away from home, a place for chatting with friends, for relaxing, undisturbed, for hours on end. Gossip is exchanged, problems pondered, all between sips of aromatic coffee. Many kinds are served, the most famous of which is Kaffee mit Schlag, strong coffee smothered with generous dollops of whipped cream.

Coffee in Vienna is seldom enjoyed without a sweet accompaniment. Ever since sugar became widely available in Europe in the early nineteenth century, Austrians have excelled in pastry making, raising it to an art form and a passion. Nowhere else in the world are there such a unique variety of cakes, pastries, strudels, and cookies as in this dessert lover's paradise. Four o'clock in the afternoon signals a special ritual. A snowy cloth is spread, fine china set, and the table laden with an assortment of freshly baked treats. Desserts are the high point of every meal. Austrians can conceive of a dinner without an appetizer but never of a dinner without a sweet conclusion.

In coming to America and establishing Viennese cuisine here, we have endeavored to carry on this great tradition. Here is a sampling of some of our most sophisticated, luscious, and dazzling desserts. Many are surprisingly light and easy—no one need forgo the fabulous experience of a Viennese dessert.

A note to the cook: never use salted butter in our recipes. You will also want to keep lots of vanilla sugar at hand!

VANILLA SUGAR

Vanilla Sugar is a staple in Austrian desserts. Here's a simple way to make your own.

5 pounds sugar
4 vanilla pods

1. Pour the sugar into a large jar that will hold it all. Stick in the vanilla pods so they're covered with sugar.
2. Cover tightly and wait at least one week before using.

PRALINE PARFAIT

SERVES 12

A bite of this satiny mélange of hazelnuts, dark chocolate, cognac, and cream is conducive to ecstasy! No special equipment is needed for this ultimate frozen treat. It is simple to make and can be done a day or two in advance.

1 cup heavy cream
6 ounces sweet dark chocolate
3 eggs
1/2 cup less 1 tablespoon granulated sugar
1/2 cup less 1 tablespoon praline paste
1/3 cup cognac or brandy

1. Whip the cream in a large, chilled metal bowl and set aside.
2. Melt the chocolate in a double boiler and allow to cool slightly.
3. Meanwhile, combine the eggs and sugar in a bowl and beat until frothy. Beat in the praline paste and melted chocolate.
4. Stir the chocolate-praline mixture into the bowl of whipped cream. Mix in the cognac.
5. Line a 2-quart earthenware terrine with baking parchment.

Pour the mixture into the terrine and freeze. Before serving, unmold the parfait and slice it.

WARM CHOCOLATE ALMOND CAKE
(Mohr im Hemd)

SERVES 16

Pamper yourself and your guests with this rich and moist flourless confection. Serve it right from the oven in individual molds. Top with the silky chocolate sauce that follows.

1/4 pound sweet dark chocolate
8 tablespoons butter, softened, plus butter for the molds
1/2 cup granulated sugar
9 eggs, separated, at room temperature
1 cup blanched almonds, ground
7 tablespoons plain bread crumbs
Chocolate Sauce (recipe follows)
1/2 cup powdered sugar

1. Preheat the oven to 350° F.
2. Melt the chocolate in a double boiler. Allow to cool.
3. With an electric mixer, cream the butter and sugar in a very large bowl. Add the egg yolks and blend well.
4. Beat in the melted chocolate, then the ground almonds and bread crumbs.
5. In a separate bowl, whisk the egg whites until stiff peaks form, and carefully fold them into the batter.
6. Butter 16 tall individual baking molds or coffee mugs and dust with the powdered sugar. Pour in the batter. Place the dishes in a pan of hot water. Bake for 25 minutes, cover the cakes with aluminum foil, and bake 10 more minutes.
7. Serve warm with whipped cream and the following Chocolate Sauce.

CHOCOLATE SAUCE

MAKES 2 CUPS

This intense dark chocolate sauce is also perfect over ice cream and with many of our other desserts.

12 ounces sweet dark chocolate
5 tablespoons sugar
1/2 cup heavy cream

1. Melt the chocolate in a double boiler.
2. Stir in the sugar.
3. Pour the heavy cream into a pot. Add the melted chocolate and bring quickly to a boil. Remove from the heat immediately.

SALZBURGER NOCKERLN

SERVES 4

Golden peaks and gossamer clouds of meringue make this specialty named for Mozart's birthplace one of the most irresistible dessert soufflés in the world. An ethereal delight that should be served right from the oven.

4 teaspoons unsalted butter*
4 teaspoons currant or grape jelly
Whites of 9 large eggs, at room temperature
1/2 cup Vanilla Sugar (see Index)
Zest of 1/2 lemon, grated
Yolks of 4 eggs
1/4 cup granulated sugar
1/2 cup sifted all-purpose flour

* A reminder: never use salted butter in these recipes.

1. Preheat the oven to 450° F.

2. Place 4 (9-inch) oval au gratin dishes (or one large oval glass lasagna pan) on a baking sheet. In each small dish place 1 teaspoon of butter and 1 teaspoon of jelly. (If you are using a lasagna pan, smear the bottom with the butter and then with the jelly.)

3. Combine the egg whites, vanilla sugar, and lemon zest in a large metal bowl. Beat with an electric mixer at high speed until stiff peaks form.

4. Beat the egg yolks with the granulated sugar. Gently fold the egg yolks and flour into the meringue. Use a spatula to place 3 large mounds of the mixture into each au gratin dish. Smooth the surface of each and bake for 8 minutes, until puffed and golden.

5. Serve immediately. This is especially good with Vanilla Sauce (see Index), warm Chocolate Sauce (see Index) or cold Strawberry Sauce (recipe follows).

STRAWBERRY SAUCE

2 cups fresh or frozen strawberries
2 tablespoons powdered sugar
1 teaspoon fresh lemon juice
Dash of kirsch (optional)

1. Combine all the ingredients in a blender or food processor. Blend well.

2. This sauce can be refrigerated for several days.

FARMER CHEESE SOUFFLÉ WITH STRAWBERRY SAUCE

SERVES 6

Austrians love farmer cheese desserts, healthy, low in calories, and wonderfully delicious when sweetened. Accompanied by a fresh sauce of summer strawberries, this soufflé makes for an exciting dessert, perfect for a light conclusion to a meal.

4 eggs, separated, at room temperature
3 tablespoons granulated sugar
Zest of 1 lemon, grated
1 cup farmer cheese
6 tablespoons powdered sugar (about)
2 tablespoons fresh lemon juice
Butter for soufflé dish
1 pint strawberries, rinsed and stemmed

1. Preheat the oven to 350° F.

2. Combine the egg yolks, granulated sugar, and lemon zest in a bowl and beat until creamy. Press the farmer cheese through a fine sieve into the egg yolks and whip until smooth.

3. In a separate bowl, whip the egg whites, 4 tablespoons of the powdered sugar, and the lemon juice to a stiff meringue. Carefully fold the meringue into the farmer cheese mixture.

4. Butter an oval soufflé dish and sprinkle with 1 tablespoon of the powdered sugar. Pour in the soufflé mixture. Do not fill the dish higher than 1/4 inch below the rim, to allow rising. Place the soufflé dish in a pan of warm water that comes halfway up the sides and bake for 35 minutes.

5. Meanwhile, puree the strawberries in a food processor, strain, and sweeten to taste with about 1 tablespoon powdered sugar.

6. Place mounds of the soufflé on individual dessert plates and serve the strawberry sauce separately. You may also unmold the soufflé on one individual serving plate, surrounded by the sauce.

TOPFENKNÖDEL
Farmer Cheese Dumplings

A breeze to make, these plump dumplings, fragrant with vanilla, are luscious by themselves and unsurpassed served with tart Plum Sauce.

13 tablespoons butter
1/2 tablespoon Vanilla Sugar (see Index)
Zest of 1/2 lemon, grated
Juice of 1/2 lemon
1 1/4 cups farmer cheese, pressed through a sieve
2 eggs
1/4 cup fine-ground semolina
Pinch of salt
1/2 cup dry bread crumbs
3 1/2 tablespoons powdered sugar
Plum Sauce (optional—recipe follows)

1. Melt 2 tablespoons of the butter and combine with the vanilla sugar, lemon zest, and lemon juice in a bowl. Beat until frothy. Add the sieved farmer cheese and the eggs, and beat until smooth. Beat in the semolina and refrigerate for an hour.

2. Bring 2 quarts of water with a pinch of salt to a boil in a 3-quart pot. With an ice cream scoop, form 12 round dumplings. Drop them into the water and allow to simmer approximately 15 minutes. The dumplings will rise to the surface when done.

3. Meanwhile, in a sauté pan, melt the remaining butter and brown the bread crumbs.

4. Remove the dumplings with a slotted spoon and drain them. Roll the dumplings in the bread crumbs.

5. Serve 2 warm dumplings per person, sprinkled with powdered sugar. The Topfenknödel may be accompanied by the following Plum Sauce.

PLUM SAUCE

MAKES 3 CUPS

You might also want to try this colorful sauce over vanilla ice cream. Any leftover sauce can be frozen.

Juice of 1 lemon
Up to 1 cup plus 2 tablespoons sugar, depending on the
**   tartness of the plums**
1 (3-inch) cinnamon stick
2 to 4 whole cloves
2 pounds fresh, ripe plums, with pits removed

1. Bring 1/2 to 1 cup water, the lemon juice, 3/4 cup of the sugar, cinnamon stick, and cloves to a boil.

2. Add the plums and simmer, stirring constantly, until the skins are shriveled, about 20 to 25 minutes. Add more sugar to taste, if necessary.

3. With a slotted spoon, remove the plums to a bowl. Reduce the remaining liquid by half, strain, and pour over the fruit.

4. Allow to cool, and refrigerate. Serve with the Topfenknödel (see preceding recipe).

FRUCHTKNÖDEL
Fruit Dumplings

SERVES 6

Austrian dessert dumplings are made with apricots, strawberries, cherries, or plums. Apricots are particularly plentiful in Austria. In spring the Wachau region is breathtakingly beautiful with its flowering orchards, and in summer there is an abundance of golden, fragrant apricots to be used for making fine jams and desserts.

6 tablespoons butter
Pinch of salt
Zest of 1/2 lemon, grated
1 whole egg
1 egg yolk
3 cups farmer cheese
3 tablespoons sour cream
1 tablespoon powdered sugar
1 1/2 cups cake flour
12 plums, 12 apricots, or 18 large strawberries
24 cubes of sugar (optional)

FOR PLUM DUMPLINGS
3 tablespoons finely ground poppy seeds (you can use a
    mortar and pestle)
1 tablespoon powdered sugar

FOR APRICOT DUMPLINGS
3 tablespoons farmer cheese
1 tablespoon powdered sugar

FOR STRAWBERRY DUMPLINGS
5 tablespoons toasted plain bread crumbs
1 tablespoon powdered sugar

1. In a bowl, combine the butter, salt, and lemon zest. Whip until fluffy. Add the whole egg and egg yolk, and continue to beat to blend. Beat in the farmer cheese, sour cream, and powdered sugar. Add the flour slowly and beat until smooth. Allow the dough to rest for 30 minutes at room temperature.

2. Cut the plums or apricots in half and remove the pits, if necessary. If the fruit isn't sweet, place 1 cube of sugar in the hollow of each half.

3. On a marble pastry board, roll out the dough 1/2 inch thick. Using a pastry wheel, cut the dough into a grid of 5-inch squares. If you're using strawberries, make 18 (3-inch) squares.

4. Place a piece of fruit, cut side down, on each circle of dough and pull the pastry up around the fruit. Seal by pinching the pastry together.

The Dumplings can be prepared up to 3 hours ahead to this point. Refrigerate until ready to boil.

5. Bring 2 quarts of salted water to a boil. Add 8 dumplings and simmer until they rise to the top, approximately 15 minutes. Remove with a slotted spoon. Keep warm on a covered plate. Repeat with the remaining dumplings.

6. TO SERVE:

Plum dumplings: Sprinkle with the poppy seeds and powdered sugar.

Apricot dumplings: Sprinkle with the farmer cheese, pressed through a sieve, and the powdered sugar.

Strawberry dumplings: Roll in the toasted plain bread crumbs and sprinkle with the powdered sugar.

MILCHRAHMSTRUDEL
Warm Farmer Cheese and Cream Strudel

SERVES 12

Paper-thin strudel dough enfolds a vanilla-scented cream, the whole
baked with a creamy topping.

Butter to grease pan
Flour to dust cloth
4 tablespoons butter, melted
Powdered sugar
Vanilla Sauce (see Index)

STRUDEL DOUGH*
1 cup plus 5 tablespoons flour
1/4 teaspoon salt
2 tablespoons vegetable oil, plus oil to grease the dough
1 egg

FILLING
9 tablespoons softened butter
1/2 cup plus 1 tablespoon granulated sugar
4 eggs, separated, at room temperature
1 cup farmer cheese
2 cups sour cream
1/4 cup flour
Zest of 1 lemon, grated
Dash of salt
4 tablespoons Vanilla Sugar (see Index)
2 ounces golden seedless raisins

ROYAL TOPPING
1 cup milk
2 whole eggs
3 tablespoons granulated sugar

* If you do not wish to make the strudel dough, you will need:
2 packages filo dough
8 tablespoons sweet butter

1. For the dough, combine the flour and salt in a large bowl. With an electric beater, blend the 2 tablespoons oil, the egg, and 2/3 cup water. Combine with the dry ingredients, mixing to a smooth paste.

2. Throw the mixture on a table surface and knead firmly for 4 to 5 minutes, until the dough no longer sticks to the table surface.

3. Shape the dough into a round bread form, smear thoroughly with oil, wrap in a cloth napkin, and allow to rest for 20 minutes.

4. If you are using packaged filo dough, melt the 8 tablespoons of butter and set aside.

5. To prepare the filling, in a large bowl, cream the butter and granulated sugar with an electric beater.

6. Beat in the egg yolks, farmer cheese, and sour cream. Add the flour and continue beating for 1 minute. Whisk in the lemon zest and salt.

7. In a separate bowl, beat the egg whites and vanilla sugar to a stiff meringue. Carefully fold the meringue into the cheese filling. Gently stir in the raisins, and set aside.

8. For the topping, blend the milk, eggs, and sugar, and set aside.

9. Preheat the oven to 400° F. and grease a jelly-roll pan with butter.

10. Place a tablecloth over a table, dust it with flour, and roll out the dough as thinly as possible over the cloth until it becomes a translucent rectangle, about 3 × 2 feet. If using the filo dough, lay the top sheet on the tablecloth, brush with some of the 8 tablespoons melted butter, and top with next sheet. Continue through both packages (there are 4 sheets in a package).

11. Cover the dough with the prepared filling, leaving an inch border on all four sides. Fold in the left and right sides of the dough, lift the cloth, then roll the dough in the tablecloth into a strudel form.

12. Place the strudel in the prepared pan, brush with the 4 tablespoons melted butter, and bake for 10 minutes, until the strudel is crisp. Lower the oven to 350° F. Spoon the topping over the strudel and cover the strudel with aluminum foil, pierced with several holes. Bake for 30 minutes.

13. Cut the strudel into portions and serve warm, sprinkled with powdered sugar and accompanied by Vanilla Sauce.

VIENNESE CHERRY STRUDEL

SERVES 12

1 recipe strudel dough (see Index)*
6 tablespoons butter, plus butter for jelly-roll pan
1/4 cup plain dry bread crumbs
11/2 pounds fresh, ripe cherries, with stems and pits
    removed
1/4 cup granulated sugar
Flour
Powdered sugar

1. Prepare the strudel dough according to the recipe for Milchrahmstrudel, steps 1–3, or use prepared filo dough.

2. Preheat the oven to 375° F. and butter a jelly-roll pan.

3. Heat 4 tablespoons of the butter in a skillet and brown the bread crumbs over medium-high heat.

4. Place the pitted cherries in a bowl. Stir in the granulated sugar and bread crumbs with the butter they were browned in.

5. Spread a tablecloth over a table (minimum size 3 × 2 feet) and dust with flour. Roll out the dough, then carefully pull and stretch it until it becomes a translucent rectangle.

6. Spread the cherry mixture over the dough, leaving an inch border on all sides. Fold in the left and right sides of the dough, lift the cloth, then roll the dough in the tablecloth into a strudel form.

7. Slide the strudel onto the jelly-roll pan, curved into a horseshoe shape. Melt the remaining 2 tablespoons butter and brush the strudel with it. Bake for 20 to 30 minutes, until golden.

---

* If you do not wish to make your own strudel dough, you may substitute 2 packages filo dough, brushing it with 8 tablespoons sweet butter, melted, as described in the recipe for Milchrahmstrudel (see Index), steps 4 and 10.

8. Allow to cool slightly before slicing. Sprinkle with powdered sugar.

VIENNESE APPLE STRUDEL

SERVES 12

1 recipe strudel dough (see Index)*
4 tablespoons butter, plus butter for baking sheet
2 1/2 pounds red McIntosh apples, peeled, cored, and sliced
Dash of rum
1/2 cup sugar
2 tablespoons cinnamon
Juice of 1 lemon
1/2 cup plain dry bread crumbs
1 cup seedless golden raisins
1/2 cup chopped walnuts
Flour
Clarified butter, melted
Powdered sugar
Whipped cream

1. Prepare the strudel dough according to the recipe for Milch-rahmstrudel, steps 1–3, or use prepared filo dough.

2. Preheat the oven to 400° F. and butter a baking sheet.

3. Place the apples in a bowl, combine with the rum, sugar, cinnamon, and lemon juice.

4. In a skillet, brown the bread crumbs in the 4 tablespoons butter over medium-high heat and combine with the apples, raisins, and nuts.

5. Spread a tablecloth over a table (minimum size 3 × 2 feet) and dust with flour. Roll out the dough, then carefully pull and stretch it until it becomes a translucent rectangle.

* If you do not wish to make your own strudel dough, you may substitute 2 packages filo dough, brushing it with 8 tablespoons sweet butter, melted, as described in the recipe for Milchrahmstrudel (see Index), steps 4 and 10.

6. Spread the dough with the apple mixture, leaving an inch free on all sides. Fold in the left and right sides of the dough, lift the cloth, then roll the dough in the tablecloth into a strudel form.

7. Slide the strudel onto the baking sheet, curved into a horseshoe form. Brush with the clarified butter and bake for 15 minutes, until golden.

8. Allow to cool slightly, slice, and serve with a sprinkling of powdered sugar and whipped cream.

BUCHTELN

Sweet Buns

SERVES 6

A dessert of Czechoslovakian origin that evokes memories of a hearthside tea in a warm country kitchen. For a comforting indulgence, try these puffy, rum-scented yeast rolls, bathed in the golden vanilla custard sauce that follows.

1 cup plus 2 tablespoons flour
3/4 ounce yeast
31/2 tablespoons sugar, plus 1 teaspoon for the yeast
2/3 cup lukewarm milk
4 tablespoons butter, melted, plus butter for the baking
      pan
2 egg yolks
Zest of 1/2 lemon, grated
2 tablespoons light rum
Pinch of salt
Vanilla Sauce (optional—recipe follows)
Powdered sugar (optional)

1. Sift the flour into a bowl and make a well in the center. Crumble the yeast into the well and sprinkle the yeast with a teaspoon of sugar. Add 1/3 cup of the lukewarm milk and stir it into the

yeast with your finger until it reaches a sauce consistency. Do not stir in the flour. The yeast-milk mixture should form a puddle in the center of the flour. Cover the bowl with a dish towel and keep in a warm place for 30 minutes.

2. Uncover the bowl, add the melted butter, the remaining milk, the 3¹/₂ tablespoons sugar, the egg yolks, lemon zest, rum, and a pinch of salt. Work the dough with a wooden spoon until it no longer sticks to the side of the bowl. Cover again with a dish towel and place in a warm spot. Allow the dough to double in volume, about 1 hour.

3. Preheat the oven to 400° F. and butter a baking pan.

4. Take the dough and with your hands form little round dumplings, each ¹/₂ inch in diameter. Place the dumplings side by side in the buttered baking pan. The Buchteln should touch and stick together. Place the baking pan near the warm oven for 25 minutes and then bake in the oven for 25 minutes, until the buns are brown and puffy.

5. Serve warm with the following Vanilla Sauce or with a light dusting of powdered sugar.

VANILLA SAUCE
Crème Anglaise

MAKES 2 QUARTS

This sauce may be refrigerated for 6 days and reheated as needed.

10 egg yolks
1¹/₃ cups granulated sugar
1¹/₂ quarts milk
**2 fresh 10-inch vanilla beans or 2 tablespoons vanilla
    extract**

1. Beat the egg yolks and sugar until frothy.

2. In a large saucepan, heat the milk to the boiling point, remove from the heat, and whisk in the egg yolk–sugar mixture.

3. Make an incision in the middle of the vanilla beans and scrape the inside of the beans into the pot. Add the beans and stir over very low heat for 5 minutes. Never allow the sauce to boil.

4. Strain the sauce and serve warm. Or allow to cool and refrigerate. This can be kept for up to a week.

MOUSSE AU CHOCOLAT

SERVES 16

We find that blending chocolate and Vanilla Sauce (Crème Anglaise) makes a delicate, velvety mousse.

2 pounds 2 ounces unsweetened chocolate
2 1/2 cups Vanilla Sauce (see preceding recipe)
8 cups heavy cream

1. Melt the chocolate in a double boiler.

2. Allow the melted chocolate to cool slightly and whisk in the Vanilla Sauce. Cool to room temperature.

3. Whip the heavy cream. Fold the whipped cream into the chocolate–vanilla sauce mixture.

4. Distribute in individual dishes or a large oval dish and chill in the refrigerator.

VIENNESE SWEET OMELETTES

Austrians do extraordinary things with sweet omelettes. For a brunch with a difference, try these Viennese treats. Impressive yet easy to make, they're a terrific change of pace from even the most sophisticated French toast. Following a hearty vegetable soup, Austrians often make a supper of one of these magic transformations of eggs, flour, and milk.

KAISERSCHMARREN
Emperor's Whim

SERVES 4 TO 6

A light, crisp, rum-scented delight, studded with golden raisins. Serve it the classic way with the fruit compote recipes that follow.

1 cup flour, sifted
1 cup milk
4 tablespoons sugar
4 eggs, separated, at room temperature
2 tablespoons dark rum
Zest of 1 lemon, grated
Dash of cinnamon
Pinch of salt
Clarified butter
2 tablespoons golden seedless raisins
2 tablespoons butter
Powdered sugar
Cranberry, Apple, or Pear Compote (optional—recipes
  follow)

1. Preheat the oven to 350° F.
2. Meanwhile, with an electric mixer, whip the flour, milk, and 1 tablespoon of the sugar to a smooth paste. Then beat in the egg yolks, rum, lemon zest, cinnamon, and salt.
3. In a separate bowl, whip the egg whites and 1 tablespoon of the sugar to a stiff meringue. Carefully fold the meringue into the other mixture.
4. Over a medium-high flame, heat 1/3 cup clarified butter in each of two large skillets, the second of which needs to be oven-proof. Pour the batter into the first skillet (it should be about 1 1/2 inches deep) and cook on one side like an omelette, for about 10 minutes. Add the raisins and flip the omelette into the second skillet. Transfer the skillet to the oven and bake for 10 minutes.
5. Remove the omelette from the skillet and, using 2 forks, tear

the omelette into pieces. Return the torn omelette to the skillet and add the 2 tablespoons of butter and the remaining 2 tablespoons of the sugar. Cook over medium-high heat for 4 to 5 minutes, until caramelized.

6. Serve on 4 warm plates and sprinkle with powdered sugar. The Kaiserschmarren may be accompanied by one of the following compotes.

CRANBERRY COMPOTE

SERVES 10 TO 12

2 pounds granulated sugar
2 cups dry red wine
2 pounds cranberries, rinsed and drained

1. Combine the sugar and red wine in a casserole. Bring to a boil and allow to simmer, uncovered, for 15 minutes.

2. Add the cranberries and simmer, uncovered, for 10 minutes, stirring occasionally.

3. Allow to cool and refrigerate until ready to serve. (This will keep up to a week.)

PEAR COMPOTE

SERVES 4 TO 6

This may be prepared in the same way as the Apple Compote (preceding recipe), substituting 2 pounds of pears for the apples and 1/2 pint dry white wine for the same amount of water.

APPLE COMPOTE

SERVES 4 TO 6

Juice of 1 lemon
2 pounds tart apples, peeled, cored, cut into quarters and
**   then into eighths**
1/2 cup sugar
1 fresh vanilla bean
Zest of 1 lemon, grated
2–4 whole cloves

1. Combine 1 pint of water and the lemon juice in a casserole. Add the apples as you cut them up. Sprinkle with the sugar.

2. Stir in the vanilla bean, lemon zest, and cloves. Bring to a boil and simmer, uncovered, until the apples are soft, about 20 to 30 minutes.

3. Remove the apples with a slotted spoon and place in a bowl.

4. Boil the liquid until it is reduced by half. Strain it and pour it over the apples.

5. Allow to cool and refrigerate. This keeps well for up to a week.

KAPUZINER PALATSCHINKEN

SERVES 6

This is our particular favorite—crepes filled with a sumptuous chestnut puree, warmed in the oven and smoothed with our dark chocolate sauce. If the chocolate sauce makes this dessert a bit too sinful for you, try it instead topped with vanilla ice cream or freshly whipped cream sweetened with just a hint of powdered sugar.

1 cup unsweetened chestnut puree
4 tablespoons heavy cream
6 tablespoons Vanilla Sugar (see Index)
Juice of 1 lemon
12 Palatschinken (Crepes) (see Index)
2 tablespoons butter, melted
Chocolate Sauce (see Index)
Whipped cream

1. Preheat the oven to 350° F.

2. Press the chestnut puree through a sieve into a bowl and mix it with the cream, vanilla sugar, and lemon juice. Spread 2 to 3 tablespoons of the mixture on the prepared crepes.

3. Fold the crepes in half, then fold again, bringing one corner over to the other corner to form a triangle, and brush with melted butter. Place in a buttered baking dish and warm for 1 to 2 minutes in the oven.

4. Serve with chocolate sauce and whipped cream.

TOPFENPALATSCHINKEN
Farmer Cheese Crepes

SERVES 6

These traditional Austrian favorites are filled with creamy, sweetened farmer cheese and baked with a golden dome of custard. A dream of a dessert served with warm vanilla sauce.

Butter for baking dish
12 Palatschinken (Crepes) (see Index)
Powdered sugar
Vanilla Sauce (see Index)

TOPPING
2 eggs
1/2 cup milk
1/2 cup buttermilk
3 tablespoons sugar

FILLING
8 tablespoons butter, softened, plus butter for dish
Zest of 1/2 lemon, grated
6 tablespoons sugar
3 eggs, separated, at room temperature
1 cup farmer cheese
1/4 cup buttermilk
Pinch of salt
1 teaspoon Vanilla Sugar (see Index)
Juice of 1 lemon
4 tablespoons golden seedless raisins
Vanilla Sauce (see Index)

1. Preheat the oven to 400° F. and butter a deep baking dish.
2. Whisk all of the ingredients for the topping together and set aside.

3. For the filling, combine the softened butter and the lemon zest in a bowl, and beat until fluffy. Add the sugar, egg yolks, farmer cheese, and buttermilk and beat until frothy.

4. In a separate bowl, whip the egg whites, salt and vanilla sugar. Add the lemon juice and beat to a stiff meringue.

5. Carefully fold the meringue into the farmer cheese mixture and stir in the raisins.

6. Cook the crepes according to the Palatschinken recipe.

7. Spread 2 tablespoons of the filling mixture over each of the prepared crepes and roll them. Place the filled crepes in the baking dish and cover with the prepared topping. Bake for 12 minutes, until golden.

8. Sprinkle with powdered sugar and serve warm with vanilla sauce.

APRICOT PALATSCHINKEN

SERVES 4 TO 8 (2 CREPES
PER PERSON)

This luscious golden treat is easy to prepare; just fill the basic crepes with this glistening mixture of warm jam, rum, and cognac.

1/2–1 cup apricot jam, depending on number of crepes
1–2 tablespoons dark rum, depending on number of crepes
1–2 tablespoons cognac, depending on number of crepes
Palatschinken (Crepes) (see preceding recipe), as many or
     as few as you want
Powdered sugar

1. In a pan, over medium heat, warm the apricot jam with the rum and cognac.

2. Spread a generous tablespoon of the jam mixture over each crepe and roll it up.

3. Serve with a sprinkling of powdered sugar.

VIENNESE FRIED FRUITS

Use the Palatschinken batter to make these simple and treasured Austrian desserts.

SLICED APPLE FRITTERS

SERVES 6

These fritters make a terrific dessert, but are splendid as a brunch dish, served with omelettes or scrambled eggs and a side of juicy sausage. Strawberry Sauce (see Index) makes a fine accompaniment.

6 tart apples, peeled, cored, and cut into finger-thick slices
3 tablespoons dark rum
Juice of 1 lemon
3 tablespoons granulated sugar
1 teaspoon powdered cinnamon
1/2 cup oil for frying
1 recipe Palatschinken batter (see Index)
Powdered sugar

1. Marinate the apples in a bowl with the rum, lemon juice, 3 tablespoons sugar, and cinnamon for about 10 minutes.
2. Preheat the oil in a frying pan to 360° F. (It will begin to crackle. Use a fat thermometer if you want to be sure.)
3. Draw the apple slices through the prepared batter and drip off the excess. Fry until golden brown.
4. Drain on paper towels and serve with a sprinkling of powdered sugar.

SCHLOSSERBUBEN

Apprentice Locksmiths—Fried Almond-stuffed Prunes

SERVES 6

Prunes are filled with almonds, dipped in batter, and fried until golden, then rolled in shredded semisweet chocolate. Memorable with either Chocolate Sauce or Vanilla Sauce (see Index for both).

36 dried pitted prunes
36 blanched almonds
3 tablespoons dark rum
3 tablespoons granulated sugar
1/2 cup oil for frying
1 recipe Palatschinken batter (see Index)
1/2 cup cocoa mixed with 1 tablespoon sugar
Powdered sugar
Vanilla Sauce (see Index) or Chocolate Sauce (see Index)

1. Stuff each prune with 1 whole almond.
2. Marinate the prunes in the rum and 3 tablespoons sugar for 10 minutes.
3. Heat the oil in a frying pan to 360° F. (it will begin to crackle). Draw the prunes through the batter and drip off the excess. Fry until golden brown, about 2 minutes.
4. Drain the prunes on paper towels and roll them through the cocoa. Sprinkle with powdered sugar and serve with vanilla or chocolate sauce.

SACHERTORTE

One of the crowning glories of Viennese cuisine, Sachertorte is probably the best known and best loved of all our desserts. An earthly delight for the chocolate fancier, this cake was invented in 1832 by Franz Sacher, sixteen-year-old apprentice chef to Prince Metternich, the diplomat and enemy of Napoleon. Metternich was so enamored of the cake that he served it the rest of his life. The dense chocolate cake, layered with apricot jam and covered with a gleaming dark chocolate glaze, won world renown for Sacher, who went on to found the most famous hotel and restaurant in all of Vienna. The Sachertorte is a practical cake to make in advance, since it keeps for several weeks. Serve it in the approved Viennese way, accompanied by generous dollops of snowy whipped cream, a beautiful contrast with the dark chocolate glaze. It is hard to forget one's first taste of this divine cake!

9 tablespoons butter
1/2 cup powdered sugar
6 eggs, separated, at room temperature
1 teaspoon vanilla extract
4 1/2 ounces dark sweet chocolate
1/4 teaspoon salt
1/2 cup granulated sugar
1/2 cup plus 1 tablespoon sifted flour
1 cup apricot jam
Whipped cream

GLAZE
1 1/4 cups granulated sugar
9 ounces sweet chocolate

   1. Preheat the oven to 400° F. In a large bowl, cream the butter and the powdered sugar with an electric mixer. Beat in the egg yolks and the vanilla.
   2. Melt the dark chocolate in a double boiler. With the electric mixer, beat the melted chocolate into the butter–sugar–egg yolk mixture.

3. Beat the egg whites, salt, and granulated sugar to a stiff meringue. Slowly and carefully fold the meringue into the chocolate mixture. Resift the flour over the meringue mixture and gently fold in.

4. Cover the bottom and sides of a 10-inch springform cake pan with baking parchment. Pour in the cake mixture and bake for 45 minutes. Remove from the oven. Run a knife around the edge of the pan, reverse, and unmold onto a wire rack. Allow to cool.

5. When the cake has cooled, cut into 2 equal layers. Spread half of the apricot jam over one layer, cover with the other, and spread the rest of the jam over the top.

6. To make the glaze, place the sugar, 1/2 cup plus 1 tablespoon cold water, and the sweet chocolate in a pan over medium heat. Stir constantly until the sugar and chocolate have melted. Bring the glaze to 200° F. on a candy thermometer. Remove from the flame, stir with a spatula until smooth, and immediately pour over the top of the cake. The glaze will run down to cover the sides of the cake.

7. Let cool, slice, and serve with freshly whipped cream.

TOPFENSAHNETORTE
Viennese Cheesecake

SERVES 14

An incredibly light, creamy, and impressive cheesecake, perfect year round for dessert or coffee hour. This cake may take some time, but then don't many good things in life!

SHORT PASTRY BOTTOM
6 tablespoons butter, plus butter for cake pan
1 cup flour, sifted
2 tablespoons powdered sugar
1 tablespoon Vanilla Sugar (see Index)
1/2 teaspoon salt
1 egg yolk

BISCUIT CAKE
3 eggs
Zest of 1/2 lemon, grated
Juice of 1/2 lemon
3 tablespoons granulated sugar
11/2 teaspoons Vanilla Sugar (see Index)
3 tablespoons flour
2 teaspoons cornstarch
Powdered sugar

FARMER CHEESE FILLING
3/4 cup farmer cheese
7 tablespoons sugar
Pinch of salt
Juice of 1 lemon
2 tablespoons Vanilla Sugar (see Index)
2 egg yolks
11/4 cups heavy cream
3 tablespoons gelatin

FOR ASSEMBLING THE CAKE
3¹/2 tablespoons apricot jam
Powdered sugar
Seasonal fruit

1. For the pastry, preheat the oven to 350° F. and butter a 10-inch springform pan.

2. Work the 6 tablespoons butter with the flour, powdered sugar, vanilla sugar, salt, and egg yolk to make a dough.

3. Roll out the dough to fit the cake pan, pierce several times with a fork, and bake until light golden, about 30 minutes. Remove and allow to cool.

4. For the biscuit cake, keep the oven to 350° F. and line a 10-inch springform cake pan with baking parchment.

5. Beat the 3 eggs, lemon zest, lemon juice, sugar, and vanilla sugar until frothy.

6. Sift the flour and cornstarch together, slowly add to the egg mixture, and work into a dough.

7. Fill the cake pan with the prepared dough and bake for 45 minutes.

8. Remove from the oven and sprinkle the top with powdered sugar. Allow to cool, then invert on a large plate to unmold.

9. For the filling, press the farmer cheese through a sieve into a bowl. Add the sugar, salt, lemon juice, vanilla sugar, and egg yolks. Beat with an electric mixer until smooth.

10. In a separate bowl, whip the cream and set aside.

11. In a saucepan, soak the gelatin in 3 cups water and heat gently until dissolved. Slowly beat the gelatin into the farmer cheese mixture. Fold in the whipped cream.

12. To assemble the cake, spread the apricot jam over the short pastry bottom.

13. Cut the biscuit cake into 3 layers. Place the first layer on the short pastry bottom, surround with a 10-inch cake ring and top with half of the farmer cheese. Place the next biscuit layer on top and cover with farmer cheese. Close with the last layer of biscuit and refrigerate for 30 minutes.

14. Remove the cake ring, sprinkle with powdered sugar, and garnish with seasonal fruit.

LINZERTORTE

SERVES 8 TO 10

The mixture of ground nuts and flour has made the Linzertorte one of the best-loved Austrian desserts since it was first served in the early eighteenth century.

4 cups all-purpose flour, sifted
1 pound ground hazelnuts
1 pound butter
3³/₈ cups powdered sugar
1 whole egg
1 egg yolk, plus 1 egg yolk for glazing the cake
1 teaspoon powdered cinnamon
Zest of 1 lemon, grated
1 cup black currant jam

1. Preheat the oven to 350° F. and butter a 10-inch springform pan that is 2 inches high.

2. Work the flour, hazelnuts, butter, sugar, egg, 1 egg yolk, cinnamon, and lemon zest to a dough.

3. Use your fingers to press three quarters of the dough into the bottom and sides of the pan. Fill with the black currant jam.

4. Roll out the remaining dough ¹/₄ inch thick and cut into strips. Crisscross these over the filling. Beat the remaining egg yolk and brush it over the pastry. Bake for 45 minutes. Allow to cool, and unmold.

CHAPTER 11

Stocks

BROWN VEAL STOCK

MAKES ABOUT 3¹/₂
QUARTS

Brown veal stock is highly versatile and can be used successfully for all meat and game preparations. This basic stock can be made in large quantities and stored in the freezer or refrigerator.

1/2 cup oil
4 pounds veal bones, chopped into 1-inch pieces
1 cup chopped vegetables (carrots, celery, celery root
    [celeriac])
1/2 cup chopped onion
1/4 cup tomato puree
2 cups dry white wine
3 bay leaves
20 black peppercorns

1. Preheat the oven to 400° F.

2. Heat the oil in a large roasting pan and sauté the bones over high heat until browned. Place the pan in the oven for 30 minutes. Return to the stove.

3. Add the vegetables and onion, sauté over medium-high heat for 5 minutes, and return to the oven for another 20 minutes.

4. Remove from the oven, add the tomato puree, sauté over medium-high heat for 5 minutes, and then add the white wine. Reduce in the oven for 30 minutes.

5. Transfer the contents of the pan to a large pot and add 7 quarts of water. Add the seasonings and simmer, covered, for 10 to 12 hours, slowly reducing the stock by half to 3¹/₂ quarts of liquid. Skim the stock occasionally while simmering.

6. When done, strain it through a fine sieve lined with cheese-cloth. Allow to cool, then refrigerate and remove the fat once it hardens.

BROWN GAME STOCK

MAKES ABOUT 3½
QUARTS

½ cup oil
4 pounds game bones, chopped in 1-inch pieces
1 cup chopped vegetables (carrots, celery, celery root
    [celeriac])
½ cup chopped onion
¼ cup tomato puree
2 cups dry red wine
1 cup gin
1 bay leaf
20 black peppercorns
½ cup juniper berries (or ½ cup gin)

1. Preheat the oven to 400° F.

2. Heat the oil in a large roasting pan and sauté the bones over high heat until browned. Place in the oven for 30 minutes. Return to the stove.

3. Add the vegetables and onion, sauté over medium-high heat for 5 minutes, and return to the oven for 20 minutes.

4. Remove from the oven, add the tomato puree, sauté over medium-high heat for 5 more minutes, then add the red wine and gin. Reduce in the oven for 45 minutes.

5. Transfer the contents of the pan to a large pot. Add 7 quarts of water, the seasonings, and the juniper berries. Simmer, covered, for 10 to 12 hours, skimming occasionally, until the stock is slowly reduced by half, to 3½ quarts of liquid.

6. Strain through a fine sieve lined with cheesecloth. Allow to cool, then refrigerate and remove the fat when hardened.

BROWN BEEF STOCK

MAKES ABOUT 3¹/₂
QUARTS

Prepare in the same way as Brown Veal Stock (preceding recipe), using 4 pounds beef bones instead of the veal bones.

For clear beef stock, used in soups, see Bouillon in Index.

CHICKEN STOCK

MAKES ABOUT 3¹/₂
QUARTS

4 pounds chicken bones, chopped
2 cups dry white wine
1 cup chopped vegetables (carrot, celery, celery root
    [celeriac])
¹/₂ cup chopped onion
20 black peppercorns
3 bay leaves

1. Blanch the bones in boiling water for 5 minutes. Discard the water.

2. Place the bones in a large pot with 7¹/₂ quarts cold water. Add the white wine and bring to a boil. Add the chopped vegetables, onion, and seasonings, and simmer the stock, uncovered, over medium-high heat, skimming occasionally, until reduced by half, about 1¹/₂ to 2 hours.

3. Strain through a fine sieve lined with cheesecloth. Allow to cool, then refrigerate and remove the fat when hardened.

QUAIL OR SQUAB STOCK

MAKES ABOUT 3½
QUARTS

Prepare like the Veal Stock (see recipe above), substituting 4 pounds of the appropriate bones.

PORK STOCK

MAKES ABOUT 3½
QUARTS

1/2 **cup oil**
4 **pounds pork bones, chopped into 1-inch pieces**
1 **cup chopped vegetables (carrots, celery, celery root
    [celeriac])**
1/2 **cup chopped onion**
3–4 **garlic cloves, peeled**
1/4 **cup caraway seeds**
1/4 **cup tomato puree**
2 **cups dry white wine**
20 **black peppercorns**
3 **bay leaves**

1. Preheat the oven to 400° F.
2. Heat the oil in a large roasting pan and sauté the pork bones over high heat until browned. Transfer the pan to the oven for 30 minutes. Return to the stove.
3. Add the vegetables, onion, garlic, and caraway. Sauté over medium-high heat for 5 minutes and return to the oven for 20 minutes.
4. Remove from the oven, add the tomato puree, sauté for 5 more minutes, then add the white wine and seasonings. Reduce in the oven for 30 minutes.

5. Transfer the contents of the pan to a large pot and add 7½ quarts water. Slowly simmer, covered, skimming occasionally, for 10 to 12 hours, until the stock is reduced by half, to 3½ quarts of liquid.

6. Strain through a fine sieve lined with cheesecloth. Allow to cool, then refrigerate and remove the fat when hardened.

LAMB STOCK

MAKES ABOUT 3½
QUARTS

Prepare in the same way as Pork Stock (preceding recipe), substituting the appropriate bones, omitting the caraway, and adding a pinch of thyme when the stock is almost completely reduced.

FISH STOCK

MAKES ABOUT 3½
QUARTS

Prepare in the same way as Chicken Stock (preceding recipe), substituting the appropriate fish bones and heads.

Index